A Dictionary of
HOMOPHONES

By
Leslie Presson

•

Illustrated by
John LaPick

BARRON'S

Copyright © 1997 by Leslie Presson
Illustrations copyright © 1997 Barron's Educational Series, Inc.

All inquiries should be addressed to:
Barron's Educational Series, Inc.
250 Wireless Boulevard
Hauppauge, New York 11788

International Standard Book No. 0-7641-0168-4

Library of Congress Catalog Card No. 97-15368

Library of Congress Cataloging-in-Publication Data

Presson, Leslie.
    A dictionary of homophones / by Leslie Presson; illustrations by
John LaPick.
        p.   cm.
    Includes bibliographical references (p. 136).
    ISBN 0-7641-0168-4
    1. English language—Homonyms—Dictionaries. I. Title.
PE1595.P73   1997
423' .1—dc21   97-15368
                                                        CIP

PRINTED IN THE UNITED STATES OF AMERICA
9 8 7 6 5 4

Contents

The English language can be tricky for educated natives and downright treacherous for those who are new to it. Some of the most frequently confused words are homophones—words that sound alike but are spelled differently for different meanings. The spelling errors that ensue can be amusing, even ridiculous. For example: spell checkers that are designed to recognize bona fide words by spelling, not meaning, will not find *sum miss steaks four ewe.*

This easy-to-use dictionary was compiled to be a helpful resource for students of American English, writers, copy editors, and lovers of wordplay. The sentences provided for each homophone set demonstrate the correct use of each word. The entries are all words that are spelled differently: *all ways/always,* not *any one/anyone,* as well as words that have at least one accepted pronunciation that matches another, like *fate/fete, want/wont, canapé/canopy,* and *bad/bade.*

The addition of suffixes to words contributes to the mix-up, particularly when the first syllable in both words is an unstressed vowel sound, as in *affects/effects* and *allusion/illusion.* Their pronunciation in connected speech sounds similar, and for that reason they are included.

The controversy surrounding the pronunciations of *marry/merry, fairy/ferry,* and *berry/bury* and the issue of words beginning with *w* and *wh* were resolved by Kenneth G. Wilson's authoritative *The Columbia Guide to Standard American English.* His description of the regional variations that constitute Standard English and accepted usage was the basis for selecting the homophones in this dictionary.

So, when you're puzzled about *witch* word is *which,* consult *A Dictionary of Homophones* for the answer.

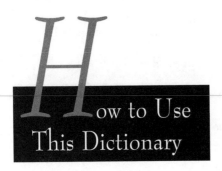

How to Use This Dictionary

The homophone (*hom-o-fone*) sets are arranged in alphabetical order, as are the many cross-referenced words. Following each entry is an abbreviation telling its part of speech, which appears in italics.

(adj.)—adjective
(adv.)—adverb
(conj.)—conjunction
(contr.)—contraction
(interj.)—interjection

(n.)—noun
(prep.)—preposition
(pron.)—pronoun
(v.)—verb

The brief definitions and the sentences are designed to help you quickly identify the most important differences between the words. For additional meanings, you should refer to a current general dictionary.

Please note that some of the illustrations show the funny mix-ups that can occur when the wrong spelling is used.

Terms A–XYZ

Abel—*(n.)* a son of Adam and Eve
able—*(adj.)* competent; skilled

>According to the Bible, *Abel* was a very *able* shepherd.

accede—*(v.)* to agree to; to assume an office or title
exceed—*(v.)* to go beyond the bounds; to surpass

>She will *accede* to the throne.
>Do not *exceed* the speed limit.

accept—*(v.)* to take; to receive with consent; to submit to; to agree to
except—*(v.)* to exclude; to take exception to; *(prep.)* but; *(conj.)* only

>I *accept* your invitation, *except* I'll be a few minutes late.

acclamation—*(n.)* a loud applause
acclimation—*(n.)* the process of getting used to the environment

>The president was greeted with *acclamation*.
>The runners needed a few days of *acclimation* before the
>big race.

acts—*(n.)* deeds; parts of a play; a book in the Bible
ax, axe—*(n.)* a cutting tool

>Splitting logs with an *ax* and then stacking them are
>vigorous *acts*.

ad—*(n.)* an advertisement
add—*(v.)* to combine; to increase; to provide

A big *ad* will *add* to your volume of business.

addition—*(n.)* the process of uniting; something added
edition—*(n.)* one of a series; the format of a work

The *addition* of pictures improved the new *edition* of the book.

adduce—*(v.)* to bring forward; to show evidence
educe—*(v.)* to draw out; to elicit; to develop

The prosecutor was able to *educe* a strong case that he could *adduce* in court.

adherence—*(n.)* a steady devotion; an allegiance or attachment
adherents—*(n.)* persons who follow a leader, cause, or idea

The cult had many *adherents* whose *adherence* was unquestioning.

ado—*(n.)* a fuss; trouble
adieu—*(n.)* a good-bye; a farewell

There will be a big *ado* when Michael bids his last *adieu*.

aerial—*(adj.)* of, in, or produced by the air; *(n.)* an antenna
Ariel—*(n.)* a sprite in a play by Shakespeare

Ariel made an *aerial* entrance in the first act.

aerie—*(n.)* the lofty nest of an eagle or a hawk
eerie—*(adj.)* uncanny; weird

Looking down from an eagle's *aerie* would give one an *eerie* feeling.

affect—*(v.)* to change; to alter; to influence; *(n.)* a state of mind
effect—*(v.)* to bring about; to accomplish; *(n.)* the result;
   a consequence

The storm's devastating *effect* will *affect* the entire region.

affected—*(v.)* changed; moved; concerned; stirred; upset; pretended;
   (adj.) insincere; phony
effected—*(v.)* brought about; accomplished

Her *affected* manner offends me.
They *effected* great changes in the city parks.

affects—*(v.)* influences; concerns; wears self-consciously; pretends
effects—*(n.)* possessions; the results

The will, listing all of his *effects*, *affects* every one of his heirs.

aid—*(n.)* assistance; help
aide—*(n.)* a helper

The class made lemonade with the *aid* of the teacher's *aide*.

ail—*(v.)* to be sick; to have trouble or pain
ale—*(n.)* a drink

You may find you *ail* in the morning if you drink too much *ale*
tonight.

air—*(n.)* a breeze; gases surrounding the earth; *(v.)* to make public
e'er—*(adj.)* ever
ere—*(conj.)* before; *(prep.)* rather than
heir—*(n.)* one who inherits

The king's *heir* was quick to *air* his excuses *ere* his subjects
could denounce him.
He spoke to them whene'er they would listen.

Your seat is on the center **aisle.**

aisle—*(n.)* a passageway between rows of shelves or seats
I'll—*(contr.)* I will or I shall
isle—*(n.)* an island

I'll sit in the *aisle* seat before we land on that *isle.*

all—*(n.)* everyone; the whole
awl—*(n.)* a small pointed tool

All of the holes in the leather were made with an *awl.*

allowed—*(v.)* permitted; provided
aloud—*(adj.)* out loud; loudly

You'll be *allowed* to read your story *aloud* in class today.

all ready—*(adj.)* completely prepared
already—*(adv.)* previously; even now

She had *already* said good-bye.
Her friends were *all ready* to leave.

alluded—*(v.)* referred to indirectly; mentioned
eluded—*(v.)* escaped from; evaded

They *alluded* to having great influence but *eluded* making a real offer to help.

Finally I was **allowed** to read **aloud**.

allusion—*(n.)* an indirect or casual reference
illusion—*(n.)* a false perception or appearance

> The magazine article made an *allusion* to how her use of cosmetics created the *illusion* of youth.

allusive—*(adj.)* making indirect references
elusive—*(adj.)* evasive; hard to grasp; baffling
illusive—*(adj.)* not real; resulting from illusion

> Her conversation was *allusive* and full of casual innuendo.
> The police searched for the *elusive* suspect.
> Don't be deluded by *illusive* advertising claims.

altar—*(n.)* a platform or table used for worship
alter—*(v.)* to change

> Candles and flowers will *alter* the appearance of the *altar*.

altogether—*(adv.)* entirely; completely; wholly
all together—*(adv.)* in a group

> When we're *all together,* our behavior changes *altogether*.

all ways—*(adv.)* by every method or direction
always—*(adv.)* every time; forever

> The dictionary is complete in *all ways* and will *always* be helpful.

amend—*(v.)* to change for the better
emend—*(v.)* to correct errors in written text

> I move to *amend* the motion on the floor.
> A copy editor will *emend* your manuscript.

analyst—*(n.)* one who analyzes
annalist—*(n.)* one who chronicles yearly events

> The nightly news *analyst* commented on the *annalist*'s report of this year's events.

I love to visit my **aunts**.

ant—*(n.)* a small insect
aunt—*(n.)* a female relative

At the picnic, my *aunt* discovered an *ant* on her sandwich.

apatite—*(n.)* a common form of calcium found in rocks, teeth, and bones
appetite—*(n.)* a desire for food or drink, or to satisfy a craving

Apatite occurs in six-sided prisms.
She had a ravenous *appetite*.

appose—*(v.)* to place next to; to juxtapose
oppose—*(v.)* to act against

I will *oppose* the plan to *appose* the new school and the jail.

apprise—*(v.)* to notify; to inform
apprize—*(v.)* to appreciate; to value

> The judge will *apprise* the court of her decision.
> We deeply *apprize* your generous contribution.

arc—*(n.)* a curved line; an arch
ark—*(v.)* a vessel; a chest

> Standing on the deck of the *ark*, Noah saw the rainbow's *arc*.

arrant—*(adj.)* incorrigible; notorious
errant—*(adj.)* wandering off; lost; mistaken

> An *arrant* drifter kidnapped the *errant* child.

ascent—*(n.)* a rising or climb up; an upward slope
assent—*(v.)* to agree; to concur; *(n.)* an agreement

> They reached an *assent* about testing the balloon's *ascent*.

assistance—*(n.)* help; aid
assistants—*(n.)* the helpers; the aides

> The patient walked with the *assistance* of two *assistants*.

ate—*(v.)* did eat; consumed
eight—*(n.)* a number following seven

> *Eight* piglets *ate* at the trough.

attendance—*(n.)* the number present; attention
attendants—*(n.)* the people who serve or are present

> The teacher took *attendance*.
> The bride and groom had four *attendants*.

auger—*(n.)* a tool for boring holes; a bit and brace
augur—*(n.)* a soothsayer; a prophet; *(v.)* to predict; to serve as an
       omen

    The *augur* told my fortune using wood shavings from an *auger.*

aural—*(adj.)* sense of hearing; of the ear
oral—*(adj.)* spoken; of the mouth

    Oral reading of fine poetry can be an *aural* delight.

aureole—*(n.)* a halo; the sun's corona
oriole—*(n.)* an orange and black bird

    During an eclipse, we see the sun's *aureole.*
    An *oriole* builds a hanging nest.

away—*(adv.)* from this place to another place; far apart
aweigh—*(adj.)* an anchor just free of the bottom

    You are free to sail *away* if the anchor is *aweigh.*

axel—*(n.)* a figure-skating jump made while turning
axle—*(n.)* the pin, bar, or shaft on which wheels turn

    He performed a double *axel.*
    The truck had a broken *axle.*

axes—*(n.)* large, chopping tools
axis—*(n.)* a central line about which an object rotates or is arranged

    The hardware store sharpens *axes.*
    The earth revolves around its *axis.*

aye (ay)—*(adv.)* yes; always
eye—*(n.)* the organ of sight; the power of seeing; an attentive look;
    an opening or section; *(v.)* to view; to watch carefully
I—*(pron.)* meaning yourself

    Aye, I have an *eye* for pretty things!

baa—*(n.)* the bleat of a sheep; *(v.)* to utter a sheep's sound
bah—*(interj.)* expression of annoyance or contempt

> A sheep's *baa* is plaintive.
> "*Bah* humbug," replied Scrooge.

bad—*(adj.)* not good; inadequate; defective; harmful; diseased; severe
bade—*(v.)* did bid

> We *bade* good-bye to *bad* winters, and moved to Hawaii.

bail—*(n.)* a payment or security to get out of jail until trial; *(v.)* to remove water; to jump out
bale—*(n.)* a large bundle; *(v.)* to make into bales

> The prisoner made *bail* with a *bale* of ten-dollar bills.

baited—*(v.)* tempted; harassed; fitted with a lure
bated—*(v.)* held in, reduced

> With *bated* breath, we tried to remove the *baited* trap.

bald—*(adj.)* hairless; plain or blunt
balled—*(v.)* made into a ball
bawled—*(v.)* cried aloud; scolded

> When he saw he was *bald*, he *bawled* out his barber.
> She *balled* the yarn for her kitten's amusement.

ball—*(n.)* any round body; a formal dance; *(v.)* to make into a ball
bawl—*(v.)* to cry aloud; to scold

The baby began to *bawl* when the *ball* rolled out of his reach.

balm—*(n.)* a soothing ointment
bomb—*(n.)* an explosive; *(v.)* to hurl or drop

No *balm* can soothe the devastation of a *bomb*.

band—*(n.)* a group; a strip or ring of metal, cloth, wood or rubber;
    (v.) to join together
banned—*(adj.)* forbidden; prohibited

A *band* of gypsies was *banned* from the park.

The **bear's** cupboard was **bare**.

bard—*(n.)* a poet, singer, or storyteller
barred—*(adj.)* striped; fitted with bars; *(v.)* excluded; prevented

Illness *barred* the *bard* from performing last night.

bare—*(adj.)* naked; empty; simple; just sufficient
bear—*(n.)* an animal; *(v.)* to carry; to give birth; to endure; to suffer

She can't *bear* seeing *bare* bodies at the beach.

baron—*(n.)* a nobleman or magnate
barren—*(adj.)* without plants; sterile; boring

After the hurricane, the *baron*'s estate was totally *barren* of trees.

base—*(n.)* a starting point; the foundation; the principal part; the bottom layer; a point on a baseball field; *(adj.)* lowly; cowardly; of little value
bass—*(n.)* a singer or musical instrument; *(adj.)* deep, low

The musician put his *bass* at the *base* of the stage.

based—*(v.)* founded on; headquartered; located at; assigned to
baste—*(v.)* to moisten while cooking; to join with loose stitches

Based on this recipe, you'll need to *baste* the roast four times.

bases—*(n.)* military installations; bottom layers; points on a playing field
basis—*(n.)* the main element; a basic fact

The *basis* of the error is he failed to touch all the *bases*.

bask—*(v.)* to lie in a warm place; to revel
Basque—*(n.)* a person living in a region in northern Spain;
       their language
basque—*(n.)* a close-fitting bodice that covers the hips

   A *Basque* from the mountains comes to *bask* on the beach.
   The *basque* she wore was laced up the front.

bazaar—*(n.)* a marketplace; a benefit sale
bizarre—*(adj.)* strange, odd; fantastic

   A *bizarre* accident occurred at our annual church *bazaar*.

be—*(v.)* to happen; to live; to continue; to exist; to become
bee—*(n.)* the insect that makes honey

   It's rewarding to *be* a *bee*keeper.

beach—*(n.)* a sandy shore; *(v.)* to ground a boat on land
beech—*(n.)* a hardwood tree

   Beech trees lined the road to the *beach*.

beat—*(v.)* to whip; to defeat; to pound or punish; to move up
      and down; *(n.)* a musical rhythm
beet—*(n.)* a dark red vegetable

   You can't *beat* pickled *beets*.

beau—*(n.)* a boyfriend, sweetheart
bow—*(n.)* a knot; a device with which to shoot arrows or play
      an instrument; *(v.)* to bend

   Her *beau* wore a colorful *bow* tie.

been—*(v.)* the past participle of *be*
bin—*(n.)* a storage box

I've *been* to the bagel *bin* too many times today.

beer—*(n.)* an alcoholic drink
bier—*(n.)* a platform for a coffin

After building the *bier*, the workers each had a *beer*.

bell—*(n.)* something that rings
belle—*(n.)* a popular female

The *bell* announced the arrival of the village *belle*.

berry—*(n.)* a small fruit
bury—*(v.)* to cover; to put out of sight

Don't *bury* ripe *berries* in whipped cream.

berth—*(n.)* a bunk; a ship's mooring; an assigned place; a safe
  distance
birth—*(v.)* being born; to create; to bring forth; *(n.)* the origin

Our cat gave *birth* to kittens in the upper *berth* of our cabin.

better—*(adv.)* more than good; *(adj.)* larger; greater; superior;
  (v.) to improve
bettor—*(n.)* one who wagers

It would be *better* if he wasn't such a frequent *bettor*.

bib—*(n.)* a cloth shield worn around the neck
Bibb—*(n.)* a variety of lettuce with small heads

The toddler wore a *bib* to eat chicken soup and a *Bibb* lettuce
salad.

bight—*(n.)* a loop in a rope; the curve of the shore; a bay or
     gulf
bite—*(v.)* to grip or cut with teeth; to annoy; *(n.)* a sting
byte—*(n.)* a group of consecutive computer bits forming a unit

    We drifted across the *bight* in our boat.
    A mosquito *bite* can get infected if you scratch it.
    There are eight bits in a *byte* of storage on a computer.

billed—*(v.)* charged; gave a statement
build—*(v.)* to erect; to establish; to create; to develop

    He *billed* his clients for materials before starting to *build* the
    house.

blew—*(v.)* did blow, spouted
blue—*(n.)* the color; *(adj.)* gloomy

    The wind *blew* her new, *blue* hat into the street.

bloc—*(n.)* a political group; people united for a cause
block—*(n.)* a city square; a solid piece; *(v.)* to obstruct

    Soldiers of the Soviet *bloc* paraded down the *block*.

boar—*(n.)* a wild hog
Boer—*(n.)* a Dutch settler in South Africa
bore—*(v.)* to drill a hole; carried; *(n.)* a dull person

    The *Boers bore* rifles when they hunted for *boar*.

board—*(n.)* a flat piece of wood; a governing group; the meals
     provided with lodging; *(v.)* to get onto a ship, train, or
     plane
bored—*(v.)* drilled; wearied; uninterested

    A *bored* member of a committee fell asleep at the *board* meeting.

boarder—*(n.)* a lodger; one who boards
border—*(n.)* an edge; a dividing line; a narrow strip

Our *boarder*'s family lives across the *border* in Canada.

bold—*(adj.)* fearless, daring; steep; clear; abrupt
bowled—*(v.)* rolled a bowling ball; moved swiftly; knocked over

The *bold*, young contestant *bowled* a perfect game.

bolder—*(adj.)* more bold
boulder—*(n.)* a large rock

The *bolder* climbers scaled the *boulder* very quickly.

bomb—*(n.)* an explosive device
bombe—*(n.)* a molded, frozen dessert

The *bomb* was hidden in a chocolate *bombe*.

Bombay—*(n.)* a seaport in West India
bombé—*(adj.)* curving outward; rounded furniture

My *bombé* desk was made in *Bombay*.

bootee (bootie)—*(n.)* a soft, knitted shoe
booty—*(n.)* the loot; the spoils of war

The baby kicked off a *bootie*.
The pirates buried their *booty*.

born—*(v.)* brought into life; created
borne—*(v.)* carried; endured; suffered

Soon after Indian babies were *born*, they were *borne* on their mothers' backs.

borough—*(n.)* a section of New York City; a town
burro—*(n.)* a small donkey
burrow—*(n.)* an animal's home; *(v.)* to dig

> The prairie dog dove into his *burrow*.
> You're not likely to see a *burro* in the *borough* of Manhattan.

bough—*(n.)* main branch of a tree
bow—*(v.)* to bend in respect; to curve downward;
    (n.) the front part of a ship

> The *bow* of his boat was tied to the *bough* of a tree on the shore.

braid—*(n.)* three or more strands interwoven; a trimming;
    (v.) to interweave
brayed—*(v.)* made the loud cry of a donkey

> The donkey *brayed* as I started to *braid* his mane.

IS THAT AN AUTHENTIC CAMEO, MY DEAR?

He **broached** the subject of the **brooch**.

brake—*(n.)* a device for slowing down; *(v.)* to stop
break—*(v.)* to crack; to burst; to disrupt; *(n.)* a happy change

You'll *break* the law if you don't *brake* at stop signs.

breach—*(n.)* a break; a gap; a violation of law or trust;
       (v.) to make a break; to fail to comply
breech—*(n.)* the back part of a gun; the buttocks

After closing the *breech* of his gun, he aimed it through a *breach* in the wall.

bread—*(n.)* a baked food; *(v.)* to coat with bread crumbs
bred—*(v.)* mated; raised, trained; brought up

A well-*bred* child will ask, "Please pass the *bread*."

brewed—*(v.)* steeped; fermented
brood—*(n.)* a flock; offspring; *(v.)* to dwell on sad feelings

Their *brood* of noisy children *brewed* a big pot of tea.

brews—*(v.)* steeps; ferments; contrives to bring about
bruise—*(n.)* surface injury; *(v.)* to hurt; to be slightly injured;
      to crush

My uncle *brews* beer at the brewery.
He suffered a slight *bruise* on his knee.

bridal—*(adj.)* of a bride or wedding
bridle—*(n.)* head harness for a horse; *(v.)* to control or
      restrain

The *bridal* party had to *bridle* their mischievous ways during the wedding.

broach—*(v.)* to risk capsizing; to start a discussion
brooch—*(n.)* a large pin with a clasp

The detective tried to *broach* the subject of the missing *brooch*.

brows—*(n.)* eyebrows; foreheads; the edges of a cliff
browse—*(v.)* to nibble; to examine casually

Above his eyes were dark *brows*.
It's fun to *browse* in a bookstore.

brut—*(adj.)* very dry, referring to wine or champagne
brute—*(n.)* a beast; a crude person; *(adj.)* not human; savage;
cruel

The *brute* drank bottle after bottle of *brut* champagne.

burger—*(n.)* a sandwich or patty made of ground meat or fowl
burgher—*(n.)* a citizen of a town

The *burgher* drank a stein of beer with his *burger*.

bussed—*(v.)* went by bus; kissed
bust—*(n.)* the chest or breast; a statue

We *bussed* to Rome to see the famous *bust* of Caesar.

but—*(conj.)* yet; except; still; nevertheless; *(adv.)* only; just
butt—*(v.)* to ram with the head; to join end to end;
(n.) the thick end; the object of jokes

He was the *butt* of their jokes, *but* he knew how to even the
score.

buy—*(v.)* to purchase; to believe; *(n.)* a bargain
by—*(prep.)* near; at; during; not later than; credited to
bye—*(interj.)* good-bye

Bye. I'm going to drive *by* a farm stand and *buy* some fresh
corn.

cache—*(n.)* a hiding place; hidden supplies
cash—*(n.)* money

In the hikers' *cache* were tins of canned food, not *cash*.

caddie—*(n.)* a golfer's attendant; *(v.)* to work as a golfer's assistant
caddy—*(n.)* a small container for tea

The golfer tipped his *caddie* well.
A silver tea *caddy* sat on the tray.

Cain—*(n.)* a son of Adam and Eve
cane—*(n.)* a walking stick; a woody stem; sugar cane; *(v.)* to weave strips of split bamboo

Cain slew his brother, Abel.
He walked with a stout *cane*.

calendar—*(n.)* a register for the days, weeks, months, and year
calender—*(n.)* a machine with rollers that smooths and glazes cloth or paper

The paper for our *calendar* was highly glazed in a *calender* at the mill.

callous—*(adj.)* unfeeling, hard-hearted
callus—*(n.)* a thick, hard place on the skin

The ballet master was *callous* about the *callus* on the dancer's toe.

canapé—*(n.)* an appetizer; an hors d'oeuvre; a small portion of food
canopy—*(n.)* a covering for shelter or protection

She was served a *canapé*.
The ceremony was held under a *canopy*.

canon—*(n.)* church law; a clerical member of a cathedral; a body of principles or standards; a comprehensive list of authentic works
cannon—*(n.)* a large piece of artillery

Priests are familiar with the rulings of *canon* law.
The *cannon* fired a loud salute.

canter—*(n.)* a smooth, easy gallop; *(v.)* to ride at a canter
cantor—*(n.)* a singer in a synagogue

The *cantor* sang as he rode and urged his horse into a *canter*.

canvas—*(n.)* a firmly woven cloth
canvass—*(n.)* a survey; *(v.)* to solicit opinions

If you *canvass* experienced campers, you'll learn about *canvas* tents.

capital—*(n.)* an uppercase letter; the top of a column; the seat of government; invested money
capitol—*(n.)* the building in which government meets

The lights from the *Capitol* dome shone down on the streets of the *capital*.

captain—*(n.)* a military officer; a leader or chief
captan—*(n.)* a fungicide used on edible plants and flowers

> The *captain* turned off the seat-belt sign.
> Use *captan* in your garden.

carat—*(n.)* a gem's weight
karat—*(n.)* the purity of gold
caret—*(n.)* a mark used in printing and writing
carrot—*(n.)* an orange root vegetable

> This is a 1-*carat* diamond in 16-*karat* gold.
> A *caret* shows where to insert a missing word.
> My rabbit likes *carrots* more than lettuce.

carol—*(n.)* a joyous song; *(v.)* to sing joyfully, especially at
    Christmas
carrel—*(n.)* a small alcove for study

> From his *carrel,* he could hear the blackbirds sing a *carol* to
> Spring.

Her friends were impressed by her 2-**carat** ring.

cast—*(n.)* a rigid dressing for a broken bone; actors in a play; an appearance or style; *(v.)* to mold; to vote; to throw; to assign a role

caste—*(n.)* social rank; a system based on social class

He wore a *cast* on his broken arm.
She wore a *caste* mark on her forehead.

caster—*(n.)* one who throws
caster (castor)—*(n.)* a small wheel on a swivel
castor—*(n.)* a beaver; a medicinal oil

With a light rod, he's a good *caster*.
The chair has a broken *caster*.
Castor oil is unpleasant to take.

caws—*(n.)* the sounds of a crow
cause—*(v.)* to bring about; *(n.)* a reason; grounds; a principle, ideal, goal

The crows' raucous *caws* can *cause* an owl to take flight.

cedar—*(n.)* a kind of tree
seeder—*(n.)* a device for sowing or removing seeds

With a *seeder,* he planted a long row of *cedar* trees.

cede—*(v.)* to grant or yield; to formally surrender
seed—*(n.)* a part of a plant; the sperm of an animal; *(v.)* to sow

If we *cede* our land to the state, we'll have no fields left to *seed*.

ceiling—*(n.)* the top part of a room; the upper limit
sealing—*(v.)* shutting tight; hunting seals; *(n.)* the closing

After *sealing* the cracks, he painted the *ceiling*.

cell—*(n.)* a small prison room; a small part of a living thing; a small unit
sell—*(v.)* to exchange for money

From his prison *cell*, he tried to *sell* his story to a publisher.

cellar—*(n.)* a basement; the space below ground level
seller—*(n.)* one who sells things

The *seller* advertised a fine, old house with a wine *cellar.*

censer—*(n.)* a container for incense
censor—*(n.)* a critic who prohibits; *(v.)* to remove from circulation
sensor—*(n.)* a device to detect and measure

Before praying, he lit the *censer.*
The *censor* thought that the book was grossly indecent.
A *sensor* turned on the lights at dusk.

cent—*(n.)* a penny coin
scent—*(n.)* a smell; *(v.)* to perfume
sent—*(v.)* transmitted; caused to go; drove

That gift of *scent*ed soap I *sent* cost more than 80 *cent*s.

cereal—*(n.)* a grain used for food
serial—*(adj.)* in a series; continuing regularly

After eating their *cereal*, they watched a morning *serial* on TV.

Ceres—*(n.)* an ancient Roman goddess; a large, bright asteroid
series—*(n.)* a sequence; a number of similar things

Ceres was the first of a *series* of asteroids to be discovered.

cession—*(n.)* a giving up, yielding
session—*(n.)* a meeting

> A treaty of territorial *cession* was announced in a *session* of the United Nations.

chance—*(n.)* luck; an opportunity; a gamble; an accident
chants—*(v.)* sings; *(n.)* simple tunes with words

> While on vacation, I had a *chance* to hear authentic Navajo *chants*.

chased—*(v.)* pursued, followed; hunted
chaste—*(adj.)* pure, modest, simple

> Bacchus *chased* after *chaste*, young maidens.

chauffeur—*(n.)* one who drives another's car
shofar—*(n.)* a ram's horn used as a musical instrument

> A *chauffeur* delivered the *shofar* to the temple.

cheap—*(adj.)* inexpensive; contemptible
cheep—*(n.)* a young bird's call

> The hungry *cheep* of baby birds arose from the *cheap* birdhouse.

chews—*(v.)* bites and grinds with the teeth
choose—*(v.)* to select; to decide; to prefer

> With my luck, I'll *choose* a pet that *chews* holes in my socks.

chic—*(adj.)* fashionably elegant
skeik (sheikh)—*(n.)* an Arab chief

> The Arab *sheik* arrived with a *chic* companion.

Chile—*(n.)* a South American country
chili (chile)—*(n.)* a hot pepper or stew
chilly—*(adj.)* moderately cold; unfriendly

 I sampled *chili* peppers on a *chilly* evening in *Chile*.

choir—*(n.)* a group of singers; a part of a church
quire—*(n.)* 24 sheets of paper

 The music for the *choir* was printed on a *quire* of heavy paper.

choral—*(adj.)* sung by a chorus; for a choir
coral—*(n.)* hard skeletons of marine growth; a color

 The book of *choral* music had a cover of *coral*-colored fabric.

chord—*(n.)* musical notes played together
cord—*(n.)* a thick string; a measure of logs; a rib in fabric
cored—*(v.)* removed from the center

> She played a sustained *chord* on the piano.
> Tie the parcel with strong *cord*.
> Baked apples should be *cored*, not peeled.

chute—*(n.)* a trough down which to slide or drop
shoot—*(v.)* to discharge; to wound; to move swiftly;
          to photograph

> Children love to *shoot* down a long, narrow *chute* at the
> playground.

cite—*(v.)* to summon to a court; to quote; to refer to
sight—*(n.)* a view; vision; *(v.)* to see; to look carefully
site—*(n.)* the location, the place; *(v.)* to place at the scene

> May I *cite* your account of the tragic *sight* at the *site* of the
> accident?

clack—*(n.)* a quick, sharp sound
claque—*(n.)* a group hired to applaud a performance

> As the singer's *claque* entered the hall, you could hear the *clack*
> of their heels on the marble floor.

clammer—*(n.)* one who digs for clams
clamor—*(n.)* an uproar; *(v.)* to raise an outcry

> A *clammer* dug five bushels of clams.
> We can't be heard over the *clamor*.

clause—*(n.)* a group of words that contains a noun and a
            verb; a part of a document
claws—*(n.)* sharp nails or pincers; *(v.)* pulls; digs; scratches; tears

> One *clause* in this contract *claws* at my rights to receive royalties.

clew—*(n.)* a corner on a sail; lines on a boat

clue—*(n.)* the information leading to a solution of a mystery; *(v.)* to provide information

> The novice sailor hadn't a *clue* about where to find the *clew* of the sail.

climb—*(v.)* to mount; to rise; *(n.)* an upward movement

clime—*(n.)* the climate; a region

> In any *clime,* it's important to *climb* with adequate safeguards.

close—*(v.)* to shut, stop, or block

clothes—*(n.)* garments; *(v.)* covers with clothing

> Her closet contained so many *clothes,* she couldn't *close* the door.

He questioned the **clause** in his contract.

coarse—*(adj.)* rough; common
course—*(n.)* a direction or route to be taken; the path or track; a program of instruction; a prescribed treatment; a part of a meal; *(v.)* to run through or over swiftly

They first filled the holes in the race *course* with *coarse* gravel.

coarser—*(adj.)* more coarse; rougher
courser—*(n.)* a swift horse; one who chases

As the jockey's lashing grew *coarser*, his *courser* ran faster and faster.

coat—*(n.)* an outer garment; a layer; *(v.)* to apply an outer layer
cote—*(n.)* a shelter for pigeons or doves

He pulled on his *coat* and went out to the dove*cote*.

coffers—*(n.)* a treasury; the funds of an organization
coughers—*(n.)* those who cough

He announced that the club's *coffers* were empty.
Loud *coughers* should not go to a concert.

collared—*(v.)* seized by the collar
collard—*(n.)* a kind of leafy green vegetable

The officer *collared* the juvenile offender.
We planted two rows of *collard* seeds.

colonel—*(n.)* a military officer
kernel—*(n.)* the seed of corn; the inner part of a nut; the most important part

A *colonel* was in command of the troops.
Not a *kernel* remained unpopped.

complaisant—*(adj.)* obliging, willing to please
complacent—*(adj.)* contented; smug, self-satisfied

The *complaisant* waiter hurried to fill our order.
A first-time champion should never be *complacent* about success.

complement—*(v.)* to make complete; *(n.)* that which perfects
           or completes
compliment—*(v.)* to praise; *(n.)* a courteous act; flattery

A bowl of flowers will *complement* a lovely table setting.
The teacher paid his students a *compliment* for their good
behavior.

complementary—*(adj.)* completes; supplies what is missing
complimentary—*(adj.)* praises; expresses courtesy or
           admiration; free of charge

A piece of fruit would be *complementary* after a rich, heavy meal.
Your second cup of coffee is *complimentary*.

consonance—*(n.)* an accord or agreement; a harmony of sounds
consonants—*(n.)* the letters of the alphabet that are not vowels

Teachers are in *consonance* that vowels be taught after *consonants*.

continence—*(n.)* a self-restraint; a temperance; the control of
           bodily discharge
continents—*(n.)* the main landmasses on the earth

The counselor spoke about *continence*.
There are seven *continents*.

coo—*(n.)* the murmur of a dove; *(v.)* to make the sound
coup—*(n.)* a successful, unexpected act or move; a daring
           deed; a blow

With a *coo* as the signal, the boys launched their *coup* against
the girls.

coolie—*(n.)* a laborer hired for work at subsistence wages
coulee—*(n.)* a deep ravine formed by running water

The *coolie* hauled baskets of rocks from the *coulee*.

coop—*(n.)* a cage or shelter for poultry or small animals;
    (v.) to confine
coupe—*(n.)* a closed, two-door car; a frozen dessert with
    toppings

She drove to the *coop* in her *coupe* to collect the day's eggs.

cops—*(n.)* police officers; cones of yarn on spindles
copse—*(n.)* a thicket of small trees

Hidden in a *copse* on the hill, the *cops* waited for the suspect.

core—*(n.)* the center; the inner or most important part;
    (v.) to remove the center part
corps—*(n.)* a group of people working together

At the *core* of the Peace *Corps* is a desire to improve life for others.

council—*(n.)* a group of people called together for discussion
counsel—*(n.)* advice; a lawyer; *(v.)* to advise

The homeowners' *council* agreed to seek *counsel*.

cousin—*(n.)* a son or daughter of an uncle or aunt
cozen—*(v.)* to cheat, deceive, or trick

My *cousin* liked to *cozen* others, and lost every friend she had.

coward—*(n.)* one who lacks courage, is shamefully afraid
cowered—*(v.)* cringed from cold or fear; crouched

In a panic, the *coward cowered* behind the door.

craft—*(n.)* an art or a skilled trade; a paper of varied color, texture, and weight; a plane, ship, or other vessel; *(v.)* to make with skill and care
kraft—*(n.)* a heavy brown paper used for bags and wrapping

He displayed samples of his *craft* on a table covered with *kraft* paper.

crape—*(n.)* a black fabric used for funerals and mourning
crepe—*(n.)* a crinkly cloth or paper; a type of rubber sole; a French pancake

The coffin was draped in *crape*.
Her gown was made of lavender *crepe*.

creak—*(v.)* to make a squeaking sound
creek—*(n.)* a small stream

The oars *creak* as we row down the *creek*.

crewel—*(n.)* a soft yarn used in embroidery; a type of embroidery
cruel—*(adj.)* mean; causing pain and suffering

The *cruel* judge said her *crewel*work was unworthy of being displayed.

crews—*(n.)* groups of people working together
cruise—*(v.)* to voyage; to move at an even speed; *(n.)* a vacation on a ship

The *crews* on *cruise* ships work very long hours.

cue—*(n.)* a signal or hint; a long rod; *(v.)* to prompt
queue—*(n.)* a pigtail; a list of computer data; *(v.)* to wait in a long line

As if on *cue*, the ticket holders formed a *queue* outside the gate.

currant—*(n.)* a small raisin or sour berry
current—*(n.)* the flow of water, air, or electricity;
       (adj.) in the present

Current law prohibits shipping *currant* bushes into some states.

curser—*(n.)* one who swears or wishes misfortune on another
cursor—*(n.)* a visual position indicator in text on a computer
     screen

The mean *curser* at the keyboard used the mouse to move the *cursor*.

cygnet—*(n.)* a young swan
signet—*(n.)* an official seal

The swans guarded their *cygnet*.
I wear my father's *signet* ring.

cymbal—*(n.)* a musical instrument
symbol—*(n.)* a sign or token; a mark or letter

A crash of the *cymbal* was a *symbol* of the concert's finale.

cypress—*(n.)* an evergreen tree
Cyprus—*(n.)* an island in Europe near Greece

Cyprus has many very old *cypress* trees.

dal (dhal)—*(n.)* a thick Indian dish made of dried peas or lentils and spices

doll—*(n.)* a small figure representing a child or other human figure

While she stirred the *dhal,* her daughter played with a Barbie *doll.*

dam—*(n.)* a barrier to hold back water; an animal mother; *(v.)* to create a water barrier

damn—*(v.)* to condemn; to censure; to doom; to curse; *(adj.)* cursed; *(interj.)* to express anger or disgust

The *dam* created a large lake.
I *damn* the forces that conspire to cause war!

Dane—*(n.)* a native of Denmark; a breed of dog

deign—*(v.)* to condescend; to give or grant

Hamlet, that famous *Dane,* would not *deign* to accept his mother's marriage.

days—*(n.)* the plural of day

daze—*(v.)* to stun; *(n.)* a state of shock

He passed through the *days* after her death in a *daze.*

dear—*(adj.)* beloved; costly
deer—*(n.)* a four-footed, woodland animal

Those who hold wildlife *dear* object to the hunting of *deer*.

dense—*(adj.)* thick, compact
dents—*(n.)* marks on the surface

The hail made a *dense* pattern of *dents* in the hood of the car.

descent—*(n.)* a coming or going down; ancestry; a downward
  slope
dissent—*(v.)* to disagree; *(n.)* a difference of opinion

There is *dissent* among skiers about what is an appropriate
descent for beginners.

"You're a **dear** to bring me my slippers."

The bully got his just **deserts**.

desert—*(v.)* to leave behind; to abandon; to run away from duty
dessert—*(n.)* the last part of a meal

Desert your diet and indulge in a rich *dessert*!

deserts—*(n.)* what is deserved; a reward or punishment
desserts—*(n.)* sweet foods

They received their just *deserts* for all their misdeeds.
It was difficult to pick only one of the tempting *desserts* offered.

deviser—*(n.)* an inventor; a contriver
divisor—*(n.)* a number in division by which the dividend is
divided

She's the *deviser* of a method of teaching division that high-
lights the *divisor*.

dew—*(n.)* droplets of mist
do—*(v.)* to act; to finish; to put forth; to meet expectations
due—*(adj.)* owed; rightful; proper; expected; *(prep.)* because of

Due to the heavy *dew*, we *do* not have to water the grass.

die—*(v.)* to stop living; to end; *(n.)* a shaping tool
dye—*(v.)* to color or tint; *(n.)* a coloring

The use of *dye* for hiding gray hair is not expected to *die* soon.

disburse—*(v.)* to pay out
disperse—*(v.)* to scatter; to disband; to break up

The crowd, waiting for the bank to *disburse* funds, was asked to *disperse*.

discreet—*(adj.)* careful, prudent; having good judgment
discrete—*(adj.)* separate, distinct; unrelated

Always cautious, he spoke *discreet*ly about several *discrete* matters.

doe—*(n.)* a female deer or rabbit
dough—*(n.)* a flour and liquid mixture for baking

The *doe* nursed five baby rabbits.
He flipped the pizza *dough*.

does—*(n.)* female deer or rabbits
doze—*(v.)* to nap; *(n.)* a light sleep

Does and their fawns *doze* in the shade of trees.

done—*(v.)* finished; performed
dun—*(n.)* a dull grayish color; *(v.)* to ask for payment of a debt

Her work was *done* well.
The store had to *dun* a few people for payment.

dual—*(adj.)* double; twofold; consisting of two
duel—*(n.)* an arranged fight between two persons or teams

> The car had *dual* tailpipes.
> The teams engaged in a *duel* for the title.

ducked—*(v.)* avoided; stooped quickly; bobbed
duct—*(n.)* a tube; a single, closed runway

> After he was *ducked* in the pool, he felt that one ear *duct* was plugged.

dyeing—*(v.)* to color with dye
dying—*(v.)* expiring; ending

> *Dyeing* Easter eggs can be artistic and fun.
> Some believe that *dying* for a cause is heroic.

"A Dual Duel"

earn—*(v.)* to gain by labor; to merit; to deserve
urn—*(n.)* a large vase

> If he's voted the most valuable player, he'll *earn* a handsome silver *urn*.

eave—*(n.)* the lower edge of a roof
eve—*(n.)* the day before a holiday; the evening

> On Christmas *Eve*, Santa must be careful not to slip off an *eave*.

edition—*see* addition

educe—*see* adduce

eek—*(interj.)* a sound made in surprise
eke—*(v.)* to barely manage; to mete out

> *"Eek!"* she screamed at the mouse.
> They were able to *eke* out a living.

e'er—*see* air

eerie—*see* aerie

effect—*see* affect

effected—*see* affected

effects—*see* affects

eight—*see* ate

elicit—*(v.)* to evoke; to draw forth
illicit—*(adj.)* unlawful; improper

Cruel and *illicit* acts can *elicit* the public's fury.

eluded—*see* alluded

elusion—*(n.)* the act of escaping; the avoidance of capture or detection
illusion—*(n.)* a false idea; an unreal perception

He created an *illusion* with blankets in his cell to aid in his *elusion*.

elusive—*see* allusive

ere—*see* air

errant—*see* arrant

ewe—*(n.)* a female sheep
yew—*(n.)* an evergreen tree
you—*(pron.)* one; anyone; people in general

You will discover a *ewe* giving birth behind that *yew*.

ewes—*(n.)* female sheep
yews—*(n.)* evergreen trees
use—*(v.)* to put into service; to employ; to treat; to consume

I will *use* a hedge of *yews* to fence in my herd of *ewes*.

exceed—*see* accede

except—*see* accept

exercise—*(n.)* active use or performance; an activity for developing the body or mind; *(v.)* to put into action; to use to develop or influence
exorcise (exorcize)—*(v.)* to drive away evil spirits by prayer; to free

The shaman will *exorcise* the demons with an *exercise* of faith.

eye—*see* aye

eyed—*(v.)* looked at
I'd—*(contr.)* I would; I should

I'd prefer not to be *eyed* too closely immediately after waking.

eyelet—*(n.)* a small hole
islet—*(n.)* a little island

He pulled the shoelace through the last *eyelet*.
We sailed by an *islet* in the channel.

faint—*(adj.)* weak; timid; *(v.)* to swoon
feint—*(n.)* a pretended attack

> The *feint* from the would-be mugger left her feeling helpless and *faint*.

fair—*(n.)* a bazaar; *(adj.)* lovely; clear; honest; blond
fare—*(n.)* the price or fee; food

> You pay a *fare* at the entrance to the *fair*.

fairy—*(n.)* a small magical being; *(adj.)* elfin
ferry—*(n.)* a boat used for crossing; *(v.)* to transport

> The *fairy* godmother used a pumpkin to *ferry* Cinderella to the ball.

faker—*(n.)* one who deceives or defrauds others
fakir—*(n.)* a Muslim or Hindu monk; a member of an Islamic religion

> A fraudulent *faker* claimed to be a dedicated *fakir*.

fane—*(n.)* a temple or church
feign—*(v.)* to pretend; to invent as an excuse

> In order to escape from going to the *fane*, he tried to *feign* illness.

faro—*(n.)* a gambling game played with cards
Pharaoh—*(n.)* the title of an ancient Egyptian king

The *Pharaoh* was the king of hearts in the game of *faro*.

fate—*(n.)* destiny; one's fortune or final outcome
fete—*(n.)* a festive celebration; *(v.)* to honor or entertain

Fate decreed that I miss the *fete* honoring my father.

faun—*(n.)* a Roman deity, half goat half man
fawn—*(n.)* a young deer; *(v.)* to show delight like a dog

The tapestry portrayed a young *fawn* at the feet of a pipe-playing *faun*.

fay—*(adj.)* elfin, elflike
fey—*(adj.)* able to see the future; supernatural

The *fay* children danced in a magic circle.
The mystic claimed to be *fey*.

faze—*(v.)* to disturb; to upset; to embarrass
phase—*(n.)* a stage; a time period; *(v.)* to adjust; to schedule

Don't let her tantrums *faze* you; it's just a *phase* she's going through.

feat—*(n.)* a notable deed
feet—*(n.)* the plural of foot; units of measurement; appendages

His greatest *feat* was vaulting the crossbar at 20 *feet*.

fends—*(v.)* wards off; resists; manages alone
fens—*(n.)* low, flat marshy areas, swamps; monetary units in China

A hearty snack *fends* off hunger.
Wild geese like to nest in *fens*.

The crowd applauded his great **feat.**

few—*(adj.)* not many
phew—*(interj.)* an expression of disgust, surprise, or relief

Phew! I found a *few* of the lost keys safe in my pocket.

fiancé—*(n.)* an engaged man
fiancée—*(n.)* an engaged woman

He introduced his *fiancée* to his mother's distinguished *fiancé.*

filé—*(n.)* an ingredient in Creole cooking
fillet—*(n.)* a boneless cut of meat or fish; an ornamental
narrow strip; *(v.)* to cut or prepare meat or fish

The gumbo with diced tuna *fillet* is flavored with *filé.*

filter—*(n.)* a substance that removes impurities;
     (v.) to penetrate slowly
philter—*(n.)* a magic potion; *(v.)* to enchant or bewitch with
     a potion

    The sorcerer prepared the *philter,* then poured it through a *filter.*

fined—*(v.)* charged money; punished
find—*(v.)* to discover; to locate; to decide

    You may be *fined* if the parking space you *find* is in a "no
stopping zone."

finish—*(v.)* to complete; to come to the end; to apply final
     touches; *(n.)* the surface coating
Finnish—*(adj.)* of or from Finland

    The *finish* on my *Finnish* furniture needs restoring.

fir—*(n.)* an evergreen tree
fur—*(n.)* the soft, thick hair of an animal

    Dressed in *fur,* she walked through the grove of *fir* trees.

fisher—*(n.)* one who fishes; a large marten
fissure—*(n.)* a crack or cleft

    The *fisher* tried to catch his dinner through a *fissure* in the ice.

flair—*(n.)* a sense of style; a talent; an ability
flare—*(v.)* to blaze up; to curve out; *(n.)* a signal light;
     an outburst

    His great *flair* for mystery caused a *flare* of curiosity.

flea—*(n.)* an insect
flee—*(v.)* to run away

    Fleas will *flee* from your dog if you use the right treatment.

flew—*(v.)* did fly; escaped
flu—*(n.)* an illness
flue—*(n.)* a chimney pipe for smoke to escape

> Our parakeet *flew* up the *flue*.
> The *flu* season lasts several months.

flocks—*(n.)* locks of hair; multitudes of people, birds or
animals; congregations; *(v.)* moves in large groups
phlox—*(n.)* a species of plant with showy flowers

> *Flocks* of deer feasted on my *phlox*.

floe—*(n.)* floating ice
flow—*(v.)* to pour out; to glide; *(n.)* the movement of a liquid

> The ice *floe* will *flow* out to sea.

flour—*(n.)* ground grain; *(v.)* to coat with flour, meal, or
bread crumbs
flower—*(n.)* a blossom; *(v.)* to reach the best stage

> Use *flour* to thicken the gravy.
> The rose bush started to *flower*.

foaled—*(v.)* gave birth to a colt or filly
fold—*(v.)* to double over; to wrap; *(n.)* a pen for sheep

> The mare *foaled* in the spring.
> Please *fold* the napkins.

for—*(prep.)* directed to; in order to; because of
fore—*(adj.)* in favor of; *(n.)* the front; *(interj.)* a call of
warning on the golf course
four—*(n.)* a number; one more than three

> *Four* citizens *for* reducing taxes brought the matter to the *fore*.

foregone—*(adj.)* having gone before or previously
forgone—*(v.)* given up; refrained from

That's a *foregone* conclusion.
Further discussion will be *forgone*.

foreword—*(n.)* the preface in a book
forward—*(adj.)* bold; eager; *(adv.)* toward the front;
(n.) a player stationed in front; *(v.)* to send ahead

Looking *forward* to the completion of his book, the author
wrote a lengthy *foreword*.

fort—*(n.)* a permanent army post; a fortified place
forte—*(n.)* a person's strong point; a specialty

His *forte* was designing impenetrable *forts*.

forth—*(adv.)* forward; onward
fourth—*(n.)* after third, before fifth

Go *forth* and march with pride on the *Fourth* of July.

foul—*(adj.)* filthy; bad; wicked; stormy; *(v.)* to entangle;
to hit outside the limits
fowl—*(n.)* birds used for food; any bird

The *fowl* were kept in a *foul*-smelling henhouse.

franc—*(n.)* a French, Belgian, and Swiss monetary unit
frank—*(adj.)* honest; open

The Minister of Finance was *frank* about the current value of
the *franc*.

The first baseman caught a **foul** ball.

frays—*(v.)* wears out, makes ragged; *(n.)* small battles; quarrels
phrase—*(n.)* a group of related words

> He *frays* his new jeans just to be fashionable.
> A *phrase* does not contain a subject and a verb.

frees—*(v.)* releases; clears
freeze—*(v.)* to become frozen; to stop movement
frieze—*(n.)* a decorative panel

> A generous grant *frees* the artist to paint the *frieze* of his dreams.
> Water will *freeze* at 0° Celsius.

friar—*(n.)* a member of a religious order
fryer—*(n.)* a chicken; a pot for frying

> The responsible *friar* prepared a *fryer* to serve to his brethren
> for dinner.

gaff—*(n.)* an iron hook for climbing or landing fish; a spar; a spur; *(v.)* to hook
gaffe—*(n.)* a social blunder

It would be a *gaffe* to present a *gaff* to someone who doesn't fish.

gage—*(n.)* a glove thrown down as a token of a challenge; a kind of plum
gauge—*(n.)* a measurement device; *(v.)* to estimate; to determine the exact measurement

It's hard to *gauge* how good the crop of green*gage* plums will be this year.

gait—*(n.)* a pace; a manner of walking
gate—*(n.)* the door in a fence

The track team advanced through the *gate* at a moderate *gait*.

gall—*(n.)* audacity; something bitter; an abnormal growth in plants; *(v.)* to chafe or rub
Gaul—*(n.)* a part of the ancient Roman Empire

He had the *gall* to say he traced his lineage back to *Gaul*.

gamble—*(v.)* to wager; to take a risk; *(n.)* a bet; a risk
gambol—*(v.)* to frolic; to skip about; *(n.)* a frolic

The lovers took a *gamble* and began to *gambol* in the fountain.

genes—*(n.)* genetic units
jeans—*(n.)* denim pants

The ability to wear tight Western *jeans* must be in your *genes*.

gibe—*(v.)* to taunt; *(n.)* a jeer
jibe—*(n.)* a sudden shift in direction; *(v.)* to be in accord

A *gibe* from the audience interrupted the speaker.
These findings do not *jibe* with the facts as I know them.

Gambling became an obsession.

gild—*(v.)* to coat with gold; to make more attractive
guild—*(n.)* an association of people

To learn how to *gild* an antique frame, you need not join a *guild*.

gilder—*(n.)* one who gilds
guilder—*(n.)* a monetary unit of the Netherlands

A Dutch *gilder*'s work is worth many *guilders*.

gilt—*(n.)* a thin coating of gold
guilt—*(n.)* the blame for a wrongdoing

The *gilt* peeled off a trophy that I won long ago.
Sometimes it's difficult to determine *guilt*.

gin—*(n.)* a liquor; a card game; a machine used to process cotton
jinn—*(n.)* a magical spirit

A *jinn* emerged from a Persian urn and poured me a jigger of *gin*.

gnome—*(n.)* an imaginary dwarf
Nome—*(n.)* a city in Alaska

The *gnome* dwelt in a cave.
We'll fly to *Nome* today.

gnu—*(n.)* an antelope
knew—*(v.)* did understand; remembered
new—*(adj.)* fresh; for the first time

I *knew* that the *gnu* was *new* to the zoo.

gofer—*(n.)* an errand runner
gopher—*(n.)* a ground squirrel

The *gofer* arrived with our lunch.
The busy *gopher* searched for seeds.

A **gofer** brought her coffee.

gorilla—*(n.)* a large ape
guerrilla (guerilla)—*(n.)* a soldier in a small, irregular force

> Modern *guerrillas* depend on guns.
> *Gorillas* are becoming endangered.

gourd—*(n.)* the fruit of a plant
gored—*(v.)* pierced by an animal's horn

> A hollow *gourd* makes a very fine ladle.
> A bullfighter risks being *gored*.

grade—*(n.)* a class in school; a degree of slope, rank, or classification; *(v.)* to change the slant or slope; to evaluate
grayed—*(v.)* became older or gray-haired

> As the population has *grayed*, some have maintained a fair *grade* of fitness.

graham—*(adj.)* made of whole wheat
gram—*(n.)* a metric unit of mass or weight

She was served a *gram* of *graham* crackers.

grate—*(v.)* to shred; to make a harsh sound; *(n.)* a metal grille
great—*(adj.)* large; fine; notable, important

Most *great* pasta recipes tell you to freshly *grate* the cheese.

grays—*(v.)* becomes gray or old
graze—*(v.)* to feed on grass; to eat lightly; to touch, rub, or scrape lightly

A sheltie will watch a flock *graze,* though it *grays* and goes lame.

grease—*(n.)* melted fat; *(v.)* to coat with oil; to lubricate
Greece—*(n.)* a country in Europe

In *Greece,* olive oil, not *grease,* is used for frying.

grill—*(v.)* to broil; to question; *(n.)* a broiled food; a restaurant
grille—*(n.)* an open framework of metal

There was an iron *grille* on each window of the *grill.*

grisly—*(adj.)* horrible, ghastly, grim
grizzly—*(n.)* a large, brown bear; *(adj.)* gray-haired, old

A *grizzly* bear is capable of *grisly* behavior.

groan—*(n.)* a deep sigh; *(v.)* to moan
grown—*(v.)* increased; matured

With a *groan,* I observed how much my girth has *grown.*

guessed—*(v.)* supposed; estimated

guest—*(n.)* a visitor

We *guessed* that the *guest* of honor was over eighty years old.

guise—*(n.)* an appearance; a style of dress; a semblance; a pretense

guys—*(n.)* supporting ropes; fellows; *(v.)* guides; steadies

Riggers in the *guise* of circus clowns tightened the *guys* of the tent.

I **groan** when I see *my* waist has **grown**.

hail—*(n.)* ice pellets; *(v.)* to greet; to salute
hale—*(adj.)* healthy, vigorous

> Even a *hale* and dedicated runner will not run in a *hail*storm.

hair—*(n.)* a threadlike growth; a very small degree
hare—*(n.)* a hopping animal

> A *hare* never needs a *hair*cut.

hall—*(n.)* a passageway; a large room
haul—*(v.)* to drag, move by pulling

> It takes strength to *haul* furniture down a long *hall*.

halve—*(v.)* to divide in half
have—*(v.)* to own, possess, get; to permit; to experience

> If you *halve* the brownie, we'll each *have* a piece.

handmaid—*(n.)* a female servant or attendant; something
        subordinate
handmade—*(adj.)* made by hand, not by machine

> Her *handmaid* wore a cap and an apron trimmed with *handmade*
> lace.

handsome—*(adj.)* good-looking
hansom—*(n.)* a two-wheeled carriage drawn by one horse

> The driver in *handsome* livery stood by his *hansom* awaiting a fare.

hangar—*(n.)* a garage or repair shop for aircraft
hanger—*(n.)* a garment holder; one who hangs on

> The *hangar* was full of planes.
> Hang your coat upon a *hanger.*

hart—*(n.)* a male deer
heart—*(n.)* a symbol of love; an organ of the body; the core; spirit or courage

> With great *heart,* the *hart* faced a hungry pack of dogs.

What a beautiful head of **hair!**

hay—*(n.)* dried plant stalks; *(v.)* to mow and dry grasses
hey—*(interj.)* a call to get attention

   Hey! The *haystack* is ablaze!

hays—*(n.)* various dried plants; *(v.)* mows to make fodder
haze—*(n.)* a smoky mist; *(v.)* to subject freshmen to humiliating
   tricks

   A farmer *hays* on dry days.
   The city was clouded in a *haze*.

heal—*(v.)* to cure or mend
heel—*(n.)* a part of the foot, shoe, or sock; a scoundrel;
   an end slice of bread; *(v.)* to tilt as on a boat
he'll—*(contr.)* he shall; he will

   He'll help me find a doctor that can *heal* the *heel* of my foot.

hear—*(v.)* to listen to
here—*(adv.)* in or on this place; at this point; now

   Here in Nashville, you'll *hear* country music.

heard—*(v.)* did hear
herd—*(v.)* to move together; *(n.)* a group

   She thought she *heard* a thundering *herd* of cattle.

hears—*(v.)* listens to
here's—*(contr.)* here is; here was

   Here's a record of what the public *hears* during a political campaign.

he'd—*(contr.)* he had; he would
heed—*(v.)* to pay attention; to take notice

   He'd only a second to *heed* their warning and avoid disaster.

heir—*see* air

heroin—*(n.)* a narcotic drug
heroine—*(n.)* a female hero

> *Heroin* is a dangerous drug.
> The *heroine* of the play was very brave.

hew—*(v.)* to chop down; to conform
hue—*(n.)* a tint of a color; an outcry

> There will be a great *hue* if loggers *hew* ancient redwood trees.

hi—*(interj.)* an informal greeting, hello
high—*(adj.)* tall; lofty; elated; rich; costly; exalted;
> *(adv.)* exceeding the common degree; *(n.)* an upper level
> on a scale

> *Hi.* Let's go swimming at *high* tide.

hied—*(v.)* hastened; sped
hide—*(v.)* to conceal; to keep secret; *(n.)* an animal's pelt

> He *hied* straight to the bank to *hide* his winnings from the others.

higher—*(adj.)* more high; loftier; further up
hire—*(v.)* to employ; *(n.)* the amount paid for services

> I will *hire* you today at a *higher* rate of pay.

him—*(pron.)* that man
hymn—*(n.)* a sacred song

> We listened to *him* explain the origin of our favorite *hymn*.

ho—*(interj.)* a cry to get attention
hoe—*(n.)* a tool for breaking up soil or mixing plaster

> *Ho!* Wouldn't you rather *hoe* than pull all those weeds in your
> garden?

hoar—*(n.)* a whitish gray appearance due to age
whore—*(n.)* a woman who sells herself for money

> Methuselah wore the *hoar* of his years.
> The *whore* offered herself for a pittance.

hoard—*(v.)* to store; *(n.)* a hidden supply
horde—*(n.)* a swarm; a crowd
whored—*(v.)* behaved like a harlot; consorted with whores

> A *horde* of bees guarded their *hoard* of honey.
> The rustlers drank and *whored* when they came into town.

hoarse—*(adj.)* having a rough, husky voice
horse—*(n.)* a large, four-legged animal

> The jockey on the winning *horse* spoke with a very *hoarse* voice.

The speaker was a little **hoarse**.

hoes—*(n.)* tools for weeding; *(v.)* cultivates; weeds
hose—*(n.)* flexible tubing; stockings; *(v.)* to wash

> The *hoes* and rakes were hung next to a coil of *hose* in the shed.

hole—*(n.)* a cavity; an opening
whole—*(adj.)* intact; complete; healthy

> A *whole* family of woodpeckers lives in a *hole* in that tree.

holy—*(adj.)* sacred; pure
holey—*(adj.)* full of holes
wholly—*(adv.)* entirely, completely; fully; totally

> They *wholly* believe that Yom Kippur is the most *holy* day of
> the year.
> She wore a *holey*, old coat.

hoop—*(n.)* a circular band; a basketball rim; *(v.)* to fasten
with a hoop
whoop—*(n.)* a loud shout, cry, or cough; an expression of joy

> The crowd let out a *whoop* as the winning basket dropped
> through the *hoop*.

hostel—*(n.)* an inexpensive lodging place; an inn
hostile—*(adj.)* unfriendly; antagonistic

> They felt that the staff at the *hostel* had been a bit *hostile*.

hour—*(n.)* 60 minutes
our—*(pron.)* belonging to or done by us

> *Our* dinner will be ready in a half *hour*.

I—*see* aye

I'd—*see* eyed

idle—*(adj.)* inactive; useless
idol—*(n.)* an object of worship; an image; a false notion
idyl (idyll)—*(n.)* a poem or prose describing a pastoral scene;
a romantic affair

The *idle* beggars waited at the foot of the steps to the *idol*.
His *idyl* described a scene that was charming and picturesque.

I'll—*see* aisle

illicit—*see* elicit

illusion—*see* allusion; elusion

illusive—*see* allusive

immanent—*(adj.)* inherent; self-contained
imminent—*(adj.)* about to happen; impending; threatening

Some doctrines are *immanent* in religious faiths and change
does not appear *imminent*.

impassable—*(adj.)* can't be passed or traveled over
impassible—*(adj.)* calm; not feeling or showing emotion

The officer's face was *impassible* when he told us the road was *impassable*.

in—*(adv.)* inside; within
inn—*(n.)* a hotel or tavern

Once *in* our room at the *inn*, we unpacked and took a nap.

incidence—*(n.)* the rate of occurrence
incidents—*(n.)* the events

The *incidence* of serious *incidents* began to escalate.

indict—*(v.)* to accuse; to bring formal charges
indite—*(v.)* to compose; to write down; to create literature

When she learned they planned to *indict* her, the reporter could no longer *indite*.

innocence—*(n.)* purity; freedom from wrong; simplicity; lack of knowledge
innocents—*(n.)* those without guilt or guile; young persons

In their *innocence*, the *innocents* thought that their teacher lived at the school and was married to the janitor.

instance—*(n.)* an example
instants—*(n.)* moments

Think of an *instance* when just a few *instants* were critical.

intense—*(adj.)* very strong; extreme
intents—*(n.)* future plans; designs

The *intense* earthquake changed the developers' *intents*.

intercession—*(n.)* a plea or prayer on behalf of another
intersession—*(n.)* a short course between regular sessions

> Thanks to my adviser's *intercession,* I was able to enroll in the *intersession.*

isle—*see* aisle

islet—*see* eyelet

it's—*(contr.)* it is; it has
its—*(pron.)* that which belongs to it

> *It's* true that the car won because *its* driver was the best.

invade—*(v.)* to enter with force and take possession
inveighed—*(v.)* protested strongly; attacked with words

> The king was eager to *invade,* but his men *inveighed* against it.

jam—*(n.)* a fruit preserve; congested traffic; *(v.)* to crowd; to squeeze

jamb—*(n.)* the side post of a doorway

The toddler's hands left raspberry *jam* on the door*jamb*.

jeans—*see* genes

jibe—*see* gibe

jinks—*(n.)* lighthearted pranks; *(v.)* to make quick, jerky movements

jinx—*(n.)* something one thinks to be bad luck; a spell; *(v.)* to bring bad luck

You may laugh at your brother's high *jinks*, but I think he is a *jinx*.

jinn—*see* gin

karat—*see* carat

kernel—*see* colonel

kill—*(v.)* to slay; to do away with; to destroy; to spoil;
  to extinguish
kiln—*(n.)* an oven for baking pottery or bricks

  We had to *kill* time waiting for the *kiln* to cool.

knave—*(n.)* a dishonest person; a rascal
nave—*(n.)* the main part of a church

  While I was praying in the *nave*, some *knave* stole my wallet.

knead—*(v.)* to work by pressing, folding, and stretching
need—*(n.)* a requirement; an obligation; *(v.)* to want
kneed—*(v.)* struck with a knee

  A player may *need* a trainer to *knead* his sore muscles if he's
  kneed and roughed up in a game.

knee—*(n.)* the joint between the thigh and the leg; shaped
  like a knee
nee—*(adj.)* born; indicates a maiden name or formerly known as

  The dancer, Markova, *nee* Mary Smith, fell and injured her *knee*.

My brother is going to **night** school.

knew—*see* gnu

knickers—*(n.)* loose trousers ending just below the knee
nickers—*(v.)* neighs like a horse

A comic in plaid *knickers* trots about and *nickers* at the patrons.

knight—*(n.)* a rank or title of honor
night—*(n.)* a time of darkness

The *knight* mounted his horse and rode into the *night*.

knit—*(v.)* to loop yarn; to join together; to wrinkle the brow;
    (adj.) tightly formed
nit—*(n.)* the egg of a parasitic louse

The broken bone was slow to *knit*.
One *nit* in your scalp is cause for concern.

knock—*(v.)* to rap, as on a door; to criticize
nock—*(n.)* a notch or groove on a bow or arrow; *(v.)* to adjust
the bowstring

> I heard a *knock* on the door.
> I saw the archer *nock* his bow.

knot—*(v.)* to tie; *(n.)* a tight fastening; a flaw in wood; one
nautical mile per hour; a tangle
not—*(adv.)* in no way

> I'm *not* sure how a square *knot* is tied.

know—*(v.)* to recognize; to understand
no—*(adv.)* not so; not at all; *(adj.)* not any; not one;
(n.) a refusal

> *No* one seems to *know* why this is so.

knows—*(v.)* understands; recognizes
nose—*(n.)* a part of the face; the sense of smell

> He has a perfumer's *nose* and *knows* what fragrances are in vogue.

kraft—*see* craft

TOO MUCH, OREGANO!

The chef's **nose knows!**

lacks—*(v.)* is deficient; *(n.)* needs
lax—*(adj.)* loose; slack

A teacher *lacks* control when the classroom rules are *lax*.

lade—*(v.)* to load on; to burden or ladle
laid—*(v.)* did lay; placed; rested

The crew hired to *lade* the cargo ship *laid* their gear on the dock.

lain—*(v.)* has rested; has remained
lane—*(n.)* a narrow road; the route

All week, that broken branch has *lain* in the far left *lane*.

lama—*(n.)* a Tibetan monk
llama—*(n.)* a Peruvian animal

A poor *lama* from Tibet fell off a *llama* in Peru.

Lapps—*(n.)* Laplanders, persons native to Lapland
laps—*(v.)* drinks; gently splashes; overlaps; *(n.)* parts of a race
lapse—*(n.)* a small error; a passing of time; a termination of a
privilege

The *Lapps* swam 40 *laps*.
He allowed his subscription to *lapse*.

lay—*(v.)* did lie down; rested; to put
lei—*(n.)* a garland of flowers

> They *lay* in the grass on the hill.
> The *lei* had a beautiful fragrance.

lays—*(v.)* rests; puts; sets in place; produces
laze—*(v.)* to idle or lounge lazily

> Our dog likes to *laze* about the yard.
> A hen *lays* eggs.

lea—*(n.)* a meadow or grassy field
lee—*(n.)* a protective shelter; the side that is sheltered

> From the *lee* of the trees, they watched the squall cross
> the *lea*.

leach—*(v.)* to dissolve and wash away
leech—*(n.)* a bloodsucker

> Drenching rain can *leach* nutrients from the soil.
> Long ago, a doctor might apply a *leech* to heal his patient.

lead—*(n.)* a heavy metal; bullets; a weight
led—*(v.)* guided; directed; lived; brought as a result

> Studies *led* to banning the use of *lead* paint.

leak—*(n.)* an accidental escape; *(v.)* to let out
leek—*(n.)* an onionlike vegetable

> A plumber can usually fix a *leak*.
> *Leek* soup is delicious.

Old pipes spring **leaks**.

lean—*(v.)* to bend or rest against; to tend to; *(adj.)* thin;
    spare; meager
lien—*(n.)* a legal claim on another's property for payment of a debt

The *lien* on my neighbor's house reflects his recent *lean* years.

leased—*(v.)* rented
least—*(adj.)* smallest or slightest

With the *least* bit of effort, I *leased* my apartment.

lends—*(v.)* loans; gives; imparts
lens—*(n.)* a curved piece of glass or plastic used in optical
    instruments; a part of the eye

A magnifying *lens lends* clarity to very small print.

lessen—*(v.)* to decrease, make less
lesson—*(n.)* something learned

> To *lessen* your fear of performing, practice between every *lesson*.

lets—*(v.)* allows; permits; rents; causes to escape
let's—*(contr.)* let us

> If our ticket *lets* us extend our visit, *let's* stay until Saturday.

levee—*(n.)* an embankment; a dike
levy—*(v.)* to fine or collect; *(n.)* a tax; the amount collected

> What was the *levy* for repairing the broken *levee* after the flood?

To **lessen** your fear of performing, practice between every **lesson**.

liar—*(n.)* one who lies
lyre—*(n.)* a small, ancient harp

That *liar* says he owns a *lyre*, but I do not believe him.

lichen—*(n.)* a mosslike plant
liken—*(v.)* to compare

Lichen grows in patches on rocks.
I'd *liken* him to a squirrel.

lie—*(v.)* to tell a falsehood; to recline; *(n.)* an untruth
lye—*(n.)* a strong, alkaline substance

It would be a *lie* to say that *lye* is not a caustic substance.

limb—*(n.)* an arm, leg, or wing; a large branch of a tree
limn—*(v.)* to paint or draw; to describe

A fearless child might *limn* perched on the *limb* of a tree.

links—*(n.)* loops of a chain; a golf course; *(v.)* joins; connects
lynx—*(n.)* a wildcat with tufted ears

The *links* in the chain were not strong enough to restrain the *lynx*.

literal—*(adj.)* true to fact; strictly interpreted
littoral—*(adj.)* on the shore of a body of water

The surveyor's plan gave us a *literal* description of our property's *littoral* boundary.

lo—*(interj.)* look! see! behold
low—*(adj.)* not high or tall; deep; mean; below the normal level

Lo! See that flock of *low*-flying swans!

load—*(n.)* a burden; a large amount; *(v.)* to transfer
lode—*(n.)* a metal deposit in the earth; a rich supply
lowed—*(v.)* made the sound of cattle

> A crane was used to *load* the ore from the rich *lode* onto trucks.
> The cows *lowed* as they settled in their stalls.

loan—*(v.)* to lend; *(n.)* what was borrowed
lone—*(adj.)* alone; apart; single

> A *lone* investor was willing to *loan* me the money I needed.

loath—*(adj.)* unwilling; reluctant
loathe—*(v.)* to detest, abhor; to feel disgust

> I *loathe* someone who is *loath* to admit a gross error.

lochs—*(n.)* lakes
locks—*(n.)* devices for securing; gates for changing water
　　　　depth; curls of hair; *(v.)* fastens; links; jams together
lox—*(n.)* smoked salmon; rocket fuel

> A waitress with raven *locks* served my order of bagels and *lox*.
> Scotland has many large, deep *lochs*.

loot—*(v.)* to plunder; *(n.)* stolen goods
lute—*(n.)* an ancient stringed instrument

> The robber's *loot* included three guitars and a *lute*.

lumbar—*(adj.)* of or near the loins
lumber—*(n.)* timber sawed into boards; *(v.)* to cut timber;
　　　　to move heavily and noisily

> After breaking a *lumbar* vertebra, he could barely *lumber* along.

made—*(v.)* prepared; created; did; caused; appointed; induced; produced

maid—*(n.)* a servant; a young woman

The hotel *maid made* our beds.

mail—*(n.)* postal material; the fabric of a knight's armor; *(v.)* to send

male—*(n.)* the masculine sex

This *mail* is addressed to your *male* companion.

The **mail**box was full.

main—*(n.)* the chief part; the open ocean; *(adj.)* most
     important; utmost
mane—*(n.)* the long hair on an animal's neck
Maine—*(n.)* a New England state

    The lion's *mane* is one of his *main* physical features.
    Maine produces potatoes, lobsters, and wild blueberries.

maize—*(n.)* corn; a pale, yellow color
maze—*(n.)* a confusing network

    I wonder if playful Indian youths ever planted *maize* in a *maze*.

mall—*(n.)* a shopping center; a shaded walk
maul—*(n.)* a heavy mallet; *(v.)* to injure; to handle roughly

    A vicious dog could *maul* someone if allowed to run free in a *mall*.

manner—*(n.)* a method; a way of acting
manor—*(n.)* the main house on an estate; the estate

    We were greeted in a friendly *manner* by the lord of the *manor*.

mantel—*(n.)* the shelf above or the front of a fireplace
mantle—*(n.)* a cloak; *(v.)* to cover

    Above the *mantel* hung a portrait of a lady in a crimson *mantle*.

marc—*(n.)* a brandy; the residue after grapes have been squeezed
mark—*(n.)* a spot or scratch; an imprint; a sign or symbol; a
    target; German money; *(v.)* to show; to set off; to take
    notice of; to rate

    The bottle of *marc* bore the *mark* of the winery.

marry—*(v.)* to wed; to join; to unite
Mary—*(n.)* a girl's name
merry—*(adj.)* lively; full of fun

    We'll have a *merry* celebration when *Mary* decides to *marry*.

marshal—*(n.)* a sheriff; a military commander; *(v.)* to lead
martial—*(adj.)* warlike

A karate teacher is trained to *marshal* students of *martial* arts.

marten—*(n.)* a weasel-like animal; its fur
martin—*(n.)* a bird, a swallow

A *marten* has soft, glossy fur.
We purchased a purple *martin* house.

massed—*(adj.)* gathered in a large group
mast—*(n.)* a tall, upright pole; a spar; nuts of forest trees
used as food

The *massed* clouds hid the sun.
The boat's *mast* was made of aluminum.

mat—*(n.)* a piece of fabric or pad used as a protective cover;
material serving as a picture border; a thick tangled
mass; *(v.)* to cover; to interweave; to frame
matte—*(adj.)* having a dull surface or finish

The picture had a white *mat* in a silver frame with a *matte* finish.

mean—*(v.)* to intend; *(adj.)* unkind; stingy; degraded;
(n.) the middle; average
mien—*(n.)* manner; bearing

Just because one has a noble *mien* does not *mean* that he's noble.

meat—*(n.)* food; the edible part of a nut
meet—*(v.)* to be introduced; to assemble; to be present; to fulfill
mete—*(v.)* to pass out, distribute

Let's *meet* at a cafeteria where they *mete* out big servings of
meat and vegetables.

medal—*(n.)* an award or decoration
meddle—*(v.)* to interfere; to tamper

Don't expect a *medal* if you *meddle* in others' affairs.

melee—*(n.)* a confused fight; a hand-to-hand struggle
Malay—*(n.)* a peninsula of Thailand

We read about the ugly *melee* in *Malay*.

metal—*(n.)* an element like gold, iron, brass, or copper
mettle—*(n.)* courage; spirit

The *metal*workers displayed their *mettle* as they negotiated a new contract.

mewl—*(v.)* to cry like a newborn baby; to whimper
mule—*(n.)* the animal offspring of a mare and a donkey;
a slipper

The youngster began to *mewl* when he was denied a ride on a *mule*.

mews—*(n.)* the cries of cats or gulls; British stables; cages for hawks; a secluded street; *(v.)* to molt
muse—*(v.)* to meditate; to reflect; *(n.)* a goddess of the arts; a poet's or artist's inspiration

A statue of the *muse* Thalia stood at the gate to the *mews*.

might—*(v.)* may; *(n.)* power; strength
mite—*(n.)* a tiny insect; a very small creature or amount

You *might* be surprised if a birthday gift comes a *mite* early.

mil—*(n.)* a unit of length equal to 0.001 of an inch
mill—*(n.)* a factory; *(v.)* to grind; to move about in a crowd

A *mil* is critical when you *mill* the bore of a gun barrel.

SORRY WE DON'T SERVE MINORS.

mince—*(v.)* to cut in small pieces; to act very daintily
mints—*(n.)* candies; herbs; places where a government makes money

Mince the onions.
Pass the *mints*.

mind—*(v.)* to obey; to care; *(n.)* thoughts; memory; opinion; intelligence; attention
mined—*(v.)* dug from the earth; was excavated; laid with explosive

The builders don't *mind* that the land had once been *mined*.

miner—*(n.)* a worker in a mine
minor—*(n.)* a juvenile person

Many a *minor* was forced to become a *miner* and work below in the mines.

minks—*(n.)* small, fur-bearing animals
minx—*(n.)* a pert, flirtatious girl

> A pretty, young *minx* in the shop showed us the pelts of soft, brown *minks*.

missal—*(n.)* a book of prayers
missile—*(n.)* a weapon fired toward a target

> Turn to page eight in the *missal*.
> The *missile* destroyed its target.

missed—*(v.)* failed to hit, meet, do, attend, see, or hear
mist—*(v.)* to spray with water; *(n.)* a thin fog; water vapor

> Due to the heavy *mist*, we *missed* a left turn in the road.

moan—*(n.)* a low, sad cry; *(v.)* to complain
mown—*(v.)* was mowed; was destroyed

> She let out a *moan* when she saw that her flower bed had been *mown*.

moat—*(n.)* a ditch dug for defense
mote—*(n.)* a tiny speck of dust

> The *moat* around the castle was empty.
> I think I have a *mote* in my eye.

mode—*(n.)* style; fashion; a manner of acting or doing; a method
mowed—*(v.)* cut down grass or grain

> Flying is a modern *mode* of transportation.
> She *mowed* the lawn.

mooed—*(v.)* made the sound of a cow
mood—*(n.)* an attitude; an emotional tone or outlook; a frame
of mind

The cows at the petting zoo *mooed* at the children.
Our guests were in a festive *mood.*

moose—*(n.)* a large animal living in Northern regions
mousse—*(n.)* a light, airy food, usually a dessert; a hair
dressing

Avoid hitting a *moose* at all costs.
We ordered chocolate *mousse.*

morning—*(n.)* the first part of the day
mourning—*(v.)* showing grief

The Seven Dwarfs stood silently from *morning* till night
mourning Snow White.

mucous—*(adj.)* secreting mucus; slimy
mucus—*(n.)* the thick substance secreted for moistening and
protection

The *mucus* secreted by *mucous* membranes protects and lubricates.

muscle—*(n.)* strength; an organ of the body
mussel—*(n.)* a shellfish

A tiny *muscle* in the shell of the *mussel* is released when
cooked.

mussed—*(v.)* made messy; rumpled; *(n.)* a state of disorder
must—*(v.)* used to express necessity, probability, or certainty;
(n.) mold

My hair is badly *mussed,* so I *must* find my comb.

mustard—*(n.)* a spicy yellow condiment; a plant with yellow
      flowers

mustered—*(v.)* enlisted; gathered; assembled

The men *mustered* at the canteen for hot dogs with ketchup
and *mustard*.

Navel oranges are the best.

naval—*(adj.)* of or for a navy
navel—*(n.)* the belly button; the central point or middle

> She went to the *Naval* Academy.
> A *navel* orange is easy to peel.

nave—*see* knave

nay—*(adv.)* not only but also; indeed; *(n.)* a negative vote
neigh—*(n.)* the whinny of a horse; *(v.)* to utter the whinny

> The vote was ten ayes and one *nay*.
> The gelding greeted me with a *neigh*.

nee—*see* knee

need—*see* knead

new—*see* gnu

nickers—*see* knickers

nicks—*(n.)* small dents, chips, or wounds; *(v.)* injures slightly; grooves
nix—*(v.)* to veto; *(adv.)* no
Knicks—*(n.)* a New York basketball team

> Due to the *nicks* in their roster of players, the *Knicks* may decide to *nix* their trip to Japan.

niece—*(n.)* the daughter of one's or one's spouse's sister or brother

Nice—*(n.)* a city in southern France

I met my *niece* in *Nice* and we drove to Monaco.

night—*see* knight

nit—*see* knit

no—*see* know

nock—*see* knock

Nome—*see* gnome

none—*(pron.)* no one, not any, not at all

nun—*(n.)* a woman in a religious order

None of my classmates chose to become a *nun*.

nose—*see* knows

not—*see* knot

Guess which **one** of my friends **won** bingo!

oar—*(n.)* a long-handled paddle
or—*(conj.)* a word giving a choice of two; otherwise or else
ore—*(n.)* a mineral or metal for mining
o'er—*(adv.)* poetic form of over

> He used an *oar* to push off from the shore.
> You *or* I will go.
> The company mined iron *ore*.
> They searched *o'er* land and sea.

ode—*(n.)* a lyric poem
owed—*(v.)* was in debt; was indebted

> The poet said he *owed* his *ode* to Ulysses.

oh—*(interj.)* a cry of surprise, pain, sympathy or to get attention
owe—*(v.)* to be in debt

> *Oh!* I know it's good to *owe* nothing, but credit cards make that difficult.

one—*(n.)* a single thing or person; *(adj.)* united; the same
won—*(v.)* did win

> *One* of my friends *won* the lottery!

oppose—*see* appose

oral—*see* aural

oriole—*see* aureole

outcast—*(n.)* a person who is rejected; a homeless wanderer; *(adj.)* kept out of home or society
outcaste—*(n.)* an Indian person who has left or been expelled from a caste

> An itinerant drifter is an *outcast* from society.
> She refused an arranged marriage and thus became an *outcaste*.

our—*see* hour

overdo—*(v.)* to do to excess; to overindulge
overdue—*(adj.)* late; past due

> You'll be exhausted if you *overdo*.
> The library sent *overdue* notices.

overseas—*(adj.)* foreign; abroad; *(adv.)* beyond or across the sea
oversees—*(v.)* watches; manages; supervises

> He *oversees* production in our factory *overseas*.

paced—*(v.)* walked back and forth; measured the distance; set the pace; *(adj.)* rate of speed
paste—*(n.)* an adhesive; *(v.)* to stick on

The large cat *paced* in his cage.
Spread the *paste* on the back of the poster.

packed—*(v.)* placed things together; crammed; packaged
pact—*(n.)* an agreement; a contract

After the *pact* was signed, the diplomats *packed* and left for home.

paean—*(n.)* an outpouring of praise; a hymn of joy
paeon—*(n.)* a metric foot in verse
peon—*(n.)* an unskilled worker; a farm laborer

Her book caused a *paean* of praise.
A *paeon* has one long and three short syllables.
A *peon* is a person at the bottom of the social scale.

pail—*(n.)* a bucket
pale—*(adj.)* lacking color; faint; feeble; *(n.)* a fence picket

The painter mixed a *pale* shade of yellow in his *pail*.

pain—*(n.)* suffering; distress; *(v.)* to hurt
pane—*(n.)* a section of window glass

A cut from a broken window*pane* can cause considerable *pain*.

pair—*(n.)* two of a kind; a couple; *(v.)* to match up
pare—*(v.)* to peel; to cut, trim
pear—*(n.)* the fruit or tree

I will *pare* and slice a *pair* of Bartlett *pears* for dessert.

palate—*(n.)* the roof of the mouth; the sense of taste
palette—*(n.)* a painter's board for mixing colors; the range of
colors
pallet—*(n.)* a thin bed on the floor; a wooden platform

A gourmet has a discerning *palate*.
The artist mixed oil paints on his *palette*.
The forklift moved machinery on a *pallet*.

parish—*(n.)* a church district; a local church
perish—*(v.)* to die; to pass away; to disappear; to suffer ruin

A small *parish* may *perish* without support from the community.

parlay—*(v.)* to gamble; to use to achieve great gain
parley—*(v.)* to confer; *(n.)* a conference to discuss disputed
points

He hoped to *parlay* his winnings on the next race, but after a
parley with friends, he decided not to bet.

passable—*(adj.)* usable; acceptable; barely satisfactory
passible—*(adj.)* capable of feelings; emotional

The road was *passable* after the storm.
The depth of her grief was in keeping with her *passible* nature.

Memories of his **past passed** through his mind.

passed—*(v.)* went by; moved forward or through
past—*(adj.)* in time gone by; *(n.)* the history

> As he drifted off to sleep, memories of his *past passed* before his eyes.

patience—*(n.)* a calm endurance
patients—*(n.)* those getting medical care

> The *patients* waiting in the clinic were running out of *patience*.

pause—*(n.)* a brief stop; *(v.)* to hesitate
paws—*(n.)* animals' feet; *(v.)* touches roughly

> Without a *pause*, the keeper lifted the lion's *paws* to examine them.

peace—*(n.)* quiet; freedom from war; a state of harmony
piece—*(n.)* a part; a segment or an example

> After I gave them a *piece* of my mind, there was *peace* in the house.

peak—*(n.)* the high point, the top; *(v.)* to reach the top
peek—*(n.)* a quick look; *(v.)* to take a quick look
pique—*(v.)* to rouse, excite; *(n.)* resentment

> On the ride to the *peak* you can *peek* at the trails below.
> Strange behavior is sure to *pique* the curiosity of others.

peal—*(n.)* loud ringing sound; *(v.)* to ring
peel—*(n.)* the skin or rind; *(v.)* to pare; to lose a top skin layer

> I will sit and *peel* an apple while the bells of the carillon *peal*.

pearl—*(n.)* a precious bead; *(adj.)* a very pale gray
purl—*(n.)* a knitting stitch

> She knitted a *pearl*-colored sweater with a knit-two and *purl*-two stitch.

pedal—*(n.)* a foot lever; *(v.)* to press with the feet; to propel
peddle—*(v.)* to move about and sell things

> Gears help you *pedal* up hills.
> He came to *peddle* his wares.

peer—*(v.)* to look closely; *(n.)* an equal; a British nobleman
pier—*(n.)* a long dock; a column

> The spy would *peer* through binoculars until he saw his contact waiting at the end of the *pier*.

pekoe—*(n.)* a tea made from the first three leaves of the tea plant
picot—*(n.)* a small, decorative edging on ribbon or lace

The *pekoe* tea stained my lace collar with the *picot* trim.

penance—*(n.)* self-punishment; repentance for sins
pennants—*(n.)* long, tapered flags

The lad is doing *penance* for stealing the other team's *pennants*.

pend—*(v.)* to remain undecided; unsettled
penned—*(v.)* wrote with a pen

I *penned* a note to my lawyer because the settlement continues to *pend*.

pendant—*(n.)* a hanging ornament; a locket
pendent—*(adj.)* hanging; suspended

There, *pendent* from her slender throat, was a jeweled *pendant*.

pervade—*(v.)* to become spread throughout; to pass through
purveyed—*(v.)* provided food as a business; catered

News of her skill will soon *pervade* the neighborhood.
She has *purveyed* delicious feasts for years.

petrel—*(n.)* a sea bird
petrol—*(n.)* gasoline; petroleum

A *petrel* landed on the forward deck.
We filled the tank with *petrol*.

pew—*(n.)* a bench in church
pugh—*(interj.)* expressing disgust at an offensive odor

>We sat quietly in our *pew* before the service.
>*Pugh!* I smell rotten eggs!

Pharaoh—*see* faro

phase—*see* faze

phew—*see* few

philter—*see* filter

phlox—*see* flocks

phrase—*see* frays

pidgin—*(n.)* a simplified form of a language
pigeon—*(n.)* a kind of bird

>We spoke in *pidgin* English.
>A *pigeon* left a mess on the roof of my car.

Pilate—*(n.)* a Roman agent in the Bible
pilot—*(n.)* a qualified operator; a guide; a leader

>Pontius *Pilate* lived in the year 1 A.D.
>The *pilot* landed the plane.

piqué—*(n.)* a ribbed cotton fabric
piquet—*(n.)* a two-handed card game

>She played *piquet* in a cool *piqué* dress.

pistil—*(n.)* the seed-bearing part of a flower
pistol—*(n.)* a small handgun

> A bee landed on the flower's *pistil*.
> He drew a *pistol* and fired.

plaice—*(n.)* a kind of fish
place—*(n.)* a space or spot; a position; a duty; a location;
(v.) to put; to appoint; to assign

> This is the *place* where I caught a lot of *plaice*.

plain—*(adj.)* simple; clear; level; homely; *(n.)* a broad, flat,
expanse of land
plane—*(n.)* an aircraft; a flat surface; a woodworking tool;
a kind of tree; *(v.)* to glide on the surface

> It was *plain* that he knew how to handle a *plane*.

plait—*(n.)* a braid of hair; *(v.)* to braid
plate—*(n.)* a shallow dish; a smooth, flat piece of metal;
(v.) to cover with metal

> *Plait* flowers and ribbons in your hair.
> I chipped my grandmother's *plate*.

pleas—*(n.)* appeals; excuses; requests; entreaties
please—*(v.)* to satisfy; a polite request; to have the wish

> *Please*, do not ignore their *pleas* for justice in this matter.

plum—*(n.)* the fruit; a tree; a rewarding job
plumb—*(adj.)* in a straight line; *(v.)* to probe; *(n.)* a lead
weight

> She made a *plum* tart.
> A submarine can *plumb* the ocean's depths.

pole—*(n.)* a tall, round rod; an opposing point; a point of
interest; *(v.)* to push along with a pole
Pole—*(n.)* a native or resident of Poland
poll—*(n.)* a place to vote; a gathering of opinions;
(v.) to canvass; to register

The *Pole* read a sign on the *pole* that gave directions to the
polls.

pore—*(v.)* to study carefully; *(n.)* a tiny opening
pour—*(v.)* to flow freely; to rain heavily

Sweat will *pour* from every *pore* in a steam bath or sauna.

praise—*(v.)* to commend; *(n.)* strong approval
prays—*(v.)* implores; asks in prayer
preys—*(v.)* hunts for food; robs or kills

Praise can be very motivating.
A nation *prays* for peace.
An owl *preys* on mice.

precedence—*(n.)* priority in rank; ranked according to importance
precedents—*(n.)* earlier actions that establish a model or an
example

The *precedents* of the Olympics dictate that gold medal winners
take *precedence* in the parade.

premier—*(n.)* the first in importance or rank; a prime minister
premiere—*(n.)* a first performance or opening

The *premier* and his wife attended the *premiere* of the new
musical.

presence—*(n.)* being present; the immediate surroundings;
a dignified appearance
presents—*(n.)* gifts

The *presents* were opened in the *presence* of all of the guests.

pride—*(n.)* self-esteem; great satisfaction
pried—*(v.)* extracted with difficulty; snooped

He felt *pride* having successfully *pried* the secret from her lips.

pries—*(v.)* wedges open; snoops
prize—*(n.)* a reward; *(v.)* to value highly

He should win a *prize* if he *pries* open ten oysters a minute.

primer—*(n.)* an elementary textbook
primmer—*(adj.)* more prim; very proper

The youngster read from a *primer*.
Fashions are not getting *primmer*.

prince—*(n.)* a king's son; any outstanding person
prints—*(n.)* marks; designs; impressions; photographs;
　　(v.) writes; stamps; produces

The shop is selling *prints* of the handsome *prince* and his bride.

principal—*(adj.)* foremost; *(n.)* the head of a school;
　　the amount of a debt or investment
principle—*(n.)* a basic truth; a rule of law or ethics

Our *principal* spoke to the students about the *principle* of fair play.

When the paint dried she hung up her **prints**.

profit—*(v.)* to benefit; *(n.)* financial gain
prophet—*(n.)* one who predicts the future; a religious leader

One may *profit* from listening to the forecast of a *prophet*.

pros—*(n.) (abbrev.)* professionals
prose—*(n.)* ordinary language, not poetry

The workshop on writing *prose* was led by a group of *pros*.

Psalter—*(n.)* a book of psalms or sacred songs and poems
salter—*(n.)* a device for spreading salt; one who spreads salt

The congregation opened the *Psalter* and read in unison.
The *salter* followed the snowplow down the highway.

quarts—*(n.)* liquid amounts of 32 ounces
quartz—*(n.)* rock crystal

> The geologist used *quarts* of water to clean his samples of *quartz*.

queue—*see* cue

quire—*see* choir

quince—*(n.)* a hard yellowish fruit; the tree it grows on
quints—*(n.) (abbrev.)* quintuplets

> The *quints* all like *quince* jam on toast.

rabbet—*(v.)* to make cuts; *(n.)* a cut in wood
rabbit—*(n.)* a long-eared animal

> I will *rabbet* the front of the chest so the door will close tightly.
> Our *rabbit* escaped from its cage.

rain—*(n.)* drops of water; *(v.)* to pour down
reign—*(v.)* to rule; *(n.)* a period of sovereignty
rein—*(v.)* to curb; *(n.)* a leather strap

> It may *rain* today.
> The king's *reign* was very short.
> *Rein* in your horse!

raise—*(v.)* to lift; to increase; to cause to grow; to collect
rays—*(n.)* shafts of light; large, flat fishes
raze—*(v.)* to tear down; to demolish

> The sun's *rays* will *raise* your spirits.
> We have to *raze* the burned building.

rancor—*(n.)* bitter resentment or ill will; malice
ranker—*(adj.)* more offensive smelling; coarser

> With *rancor*, I told him that he was *ranker* than anyone else.

King George **reigned** over England.

rap—*(v.)* to strike; to knock; *(n.)* a quick blow
wrap—*(n.)* an outer covering; *(v.)* to enclose; to wind or fold

There was a *rap* at the door.
I must *wrap* the gifts tonight.

rapped—*(v.)* struck with quick blows
rapt—*(adj.)* engrossed; carried away by emotion
wrapped—*(v.)* wound or folded around; covered; enclosed

The conductor *rapped* his baton.
Rapt listeners were soon *wrapped* up in the beautiful music.

real—*(adj.)* true; actual
reel—*(n.)* a spool; *(v.)* to wind up; to whirl or stagger

His story is *real*; the fish broke his *reel*.

red—*(n.)* a primary color
read—*(v.)* learned from printed words; understood

Seated on a *red* couch, he *read* until midnight.

reed—*(n.)* a tall, thin grass; a musical instrument; part of the mouthpiece
read—*(v.)* to utter printed words; to gain information from print

He put a new *reed* in his clarinet and began to *read* the music.

reek—*(v.)* to smell strongly; *(n.)* a strong smell
wreak—*(v.)* to inflict damage; to express anger

A room can *reek* of smoke.
A tornado can *wreak* havoc.

The conductor **rapped** his baton.

residence—*(n.)* a place where one lives
residents—*(n.)* people who live in a place; doctors in training

The hospital provides a *residence* for all of its surgical *residents*.

rest—*(v.)* to lean or relax; *(n.)* sleep; a break; what is left
wrest—*(v.)* to pull or force away with a twist

The bully tried to *wrest* the *rest* of my things from me.

retch—*(v.)* to try to vomit
wretch—*(n.)* a miserable person

The poor *wretch* ran to the railing to *retch*.

review—*(v.)* to go over again; to evaluate; *(n.)* an inspection; a report; a journal
revue—*(n.)* a musical show with dancing and skits

The critics' *review* of a new Broadway *revue* is very enthusiastic.

rheum—*(n.)* a watery discharge from nose and eyes
room—*(n.)* an interior space; the scope for something

The *rheum* from his cold was annoying.
We painted the *room* a soft blue.

rhumb—*(n.)* a point of the compass; a proposed course
rum—*(n.)* an alcoholic liquor

They used the *rhumb* line to plot their course.
Rum is served in the islands with fruit juice.

rigger—*(n.)* one who works with ropes
rigor—*(n.)* strictness; severity; scrupulous accuracy

A *rigger* on a tall ship must work with faithful *rigor*.

right—*(adj.)* correct; fitting; *(n.)* the opposite of left; a legal
privilege
rite—*(n.)* a ritual; a ceremony
write—*(v.)* to form letters; to communicate with pen or pencil;
to compose music, poetry, or literature
wright—*(n.)* an artisan

A ship*wright* and a play*wright* should create with care.
He was the *right* person to *write* about the African *rite* of
passage.

ring—*(n.)* a piece of jewelry; *(v.)* to make the sound of a bell;
to encircle
wring—*(v.)* to squeeze and twist

She lost her favorite *ring*.
Wring out the wet laundry.

road—*(n.)* a way made for travel
rode—*(v.)* did ride
rowed—*(v.)* did go in a boat with oars

We *rode* down the *road* on our bikes.
They *rowed* down the river.

roads—*(n.)* ways; highways
Rhodes—*(n.)* an island near Greece

Many of the *roads* on *Rhodes* were unimproved.

roam—*(v.)* to wander
Rome—*(n.)* a city in Italy

It was a lovely day to *roam* the streets of *Rome*.

roc—*(n.)* in ancient lore, a big, powerful, predatory bird
rock—*(n.)* a large stone; a firm foundation; *(v.)* to move from
    side to side

> The *roc* dropped a huge *rock* on the soldiers guarding the
> castle.

roe—*(n.)* fish eggs; a kind of deer
row—*(n.)* in a line; *(v.)* to propel by oars

> Several kinds of *roe* can be used to make caviar.
> Our seats were in the second *row*.

role—*(n.)* a part to act; a responsibility
roll—*(n.)* a small portion of bread; a list; a length of paper;
    (v.) to move; to turn over; to form a ball

> She played the tragic *role* of Medea.
> The baby learned how to *roll* over.

roomer—*(n.)* one who rents a room
rumor—*(n.)* gossip

> The *rumor* is that your *roomer* is very attractive but unfriendly.

root—*(n.)* the underground part of a plant; a cause; the basic
    part; *(v.)* to dig up with a snout
route—*(n.)* a road or course for travel; *(v.)* to plan a course to
    take

> Poverty is one *root* of crime.
> We chose the shortest *route* home.

rose—*(n.)* the flower; a color; *(v.)* did rise
rows—*(v.)* uses oars; *(n.)* orderly lines

> They planted the *rose* garden in four long *rows*.

The golfer was in the **rough**.

rote—*(n.)* routine; by habit; memorized
wrote—*(v.)* did write

> We *wrote* the multiplication tables until we knew them by *rote*.

rough—*(adj.)* not smooth; noisy; rude; *(n.)* the uneven
ground by a golf course
ruff—*(n.)* a ruffled collar; *(v.)* to trump in a card game

> The painting depicted a *rough*-looking gentleman wearing a
> *ruff*.

rouse—*(v.)* to stir up, excite
rows—*(n.)* noisy quarrels

> The *rows* in our neighbor's apartment are sure to *rouse* every-
> one in our building.

rout—*(n.)* a mob; a total defeat; *(v.)* to force out
route—*(n.)* a road or course to follow; *(v.)* to schedule a path
       to follow

    The commander's bold *route* brought about the enemy's *rout*.

rude—*(adj.)* impolite; crude
rued—*(v.)* regretted; was sorry

    She *rued* the one time she was thoughtlessly *rude* to her friend.

rue—*(v.)* to regret; *(n.)* a variety of plant
roux—*(n.)* a blend of thickening agents in cooking

    If you don't add a *roux* to your gravy, you may *rue* the thin
    result.

rung—*(v.)* did ring; *(n.)* the step of a ladder or chair
wrung—*(v.)* twisted

    The bell had *rung* twice.
    He anxiously *wrung* his hands.

rye—*(n.)* a cereal grain
wry—*(adj.)* distorted; ironic

    I'll have a ham sandwich on *rye* bread.
    His *wry* smile told me that I should be suspicious.

sac—*(n.)* a pouch in a plant or an animal
sack—*(n.)* a soft bag; *(v.)* to plunder

> The bee's honey *sac* is in its abdomen.
> She dropped a *sack* of groceries.

sail—*(n.)* a part to catch the wind; *(v.)* to glide smoothly; to navigate on water
sale—*(n.)* a special offering at reduced prices; an exchange for money

> The ad said, "Every windsurfer *sail* is on *sale* today."

salter—*see* Psalter

sane—*(adj.)* sound of mind; sensible
seine—*(n.)* a fish net; *(v.)* to fish with a net
Seine—*(n.)* a river that flows through Paris

> No *sane* man would use a *seine* to try to fish in the *Seine*.

sari (saree)—*(n.)* a garment worn by women in India
sorry—*(adj.)* feeling regret, pity, sympathy

> She was *sorry* that the elegant *sari* did not fit her.

She was **sorry** the beautiful **sari** did not fit.

saver—*(n.)* a person who saves or avoids waste
savor—*(v.)* to enjoy; *(n.)* a particular taste or smell

When I retire, I will *savor* the rewards from being a thrifty *saver*.

scene—*(n.)* the setting; a place; a part of a play or film; an incident
seen—*(v.)* viewed; visited; recognized; observed; thought; found out

The road conditions at the *scene* of the crash were *seen* as its major cause.

scent—*see* cent

scull—*(n.)* a racing shell or boat; an oar mounted on the back;
　　(v.) to row with an oar from side to side
skull—*(n.)* the bones of the head

　　The rowing team bought a new *scull*.
　　The *skull* protects the brain.

sea—*(n.)* the ocean; the waves
see—*(v.)* to look; to understand; to learn; to view; to meet;
　　to visit

　　When you *see* an angry *sea*, you sense its awesome power.

sealing—*see* ceiling

The **scull** protects the **skull**.

seam—*(n.)* the place where two parts are joined together; *(v.)* to join with stitches
seem—*(v.)* to appear; to look like

I *seem* to be unable to sew a straight *seam* today.

seaman—*(n.)* a sailor; an enlisted Navy man
semen—*(n.)* the fluid from the male reproductive organ

The fertility clinic tested the *seaman's semen*.

sear—*(v.)* to char or burn; to make callous
seer—*(n.)* a prophet; one who observes
sere—*(adj.)* dry, withered

A *seer* could *sear* the hopes of his followers leaving them with visions of a *sere* world to come.

seas—*(n.)* bodies of water; the waves
sees—*(v.)* looks; views; visits; learns
seize—*(v.)* to grab; to take control; to bind

In this painting, the viewer *sees* Lord Nelson's final attempt to *seize* control of the *seas*.

sects—*(n.)* groups of specific religious faiths
sex—*(n.)* gender

Most *sects* do not discriminate on the basis of *sex*.

seed—*see* cede

seeder—*see* cedar

seen—*see* scene

sell—*see* cell

seller—*see* cellar

sensor—*see* censer

sent—*see* cent

serf—*(n.)* a slave to a landowner
surf—*(v.)* to ride on the crest of a wave; *(n.)* breaking waves

> In feudal times, a *serf* had to serve the lord of the castle.
> The *surf* crashed against the rocky shore.

serge—*(v.)* to finish the edge of cloth; *(n.)* a fabric
surge—*(n.)* a large wave; a sudden increase in intensity;
> > *(v.)* to increase suddenly

> His suit was made of brown *serge*.
> Caught in the *surge*, the small craft capsized.

serial—*see* cereal

series—*see* Ceres

session—*see* cession

sew—*(v.)* to stitch; to mend; to make
so—*(adv.)* very; *(conj.)* for that reason; then; in order that
sow—*(v.)* to scatter seeds

> She likes to *sew* her own clothes, *so* her wardrobe is unique.
> *Sow* radishes every few weeks for a continuous crop.

shear—*(v.)* to clip; to trim
sheer—*(adj.)* extremely steep; very thin; total; *(v.)* to turn
> aside; to swerve; *(adv.)* completely; utterly

> It's *sheer* nonsense to think that a child could *shear* a tall
> hedge.

sheik (sheikh)—*see* chic

shoe—*(n.)* a foot covering; a horseshoe; *(v.)* to apply shoes on
a horse
shoo—*(v.)* to drive away; *(interj.)* begone!

As he labored to *shoe* the mare, he had to *shoo* the horseflies
away.

shofar—*see* chauffeur

shone—*(v.)* glowed; stood out
shown—*(v.)* did show; exhibited

Her face *shone* with delight when she learned that her work
would be *shown* at the gallery.

shoot—*see* chute

sic—*(v.)* to cause to attack
[sic]—*(adv.)* so; thus; indicating a misspelling or misuse
sick—*(adj.)* ill; very disturbed; disgusted; impaired

Only a *sick* mind would think to *sic* a dog on an innocent
person.

side—*(n.)* the edge or margin; either half; a position;
(v.) to support; *(adj.)* at one side
sighed—*(v.)* did sigh; breathed deeply and audibly

He *sighed* when he saw that one *side* of the pancake was burnt.

sighs—*(n.)* deep loud breaths
size—*(n.)* the measurement, bulk, dimension; *(v.)* to stiffen

There were *sighs* of envy as the models paraded in *size* six
bathing suits.

sight—*see* cite

sign—*(n.)* a signal; an indication; *(v.)* to affix one's name;
to communicate
sine—*(n.)* a fundamental function in trigonometry

She gave a *sign* that she knew how to compute the *sine*.

signet—*see* cygnet

slay—*(v.)* to murder or kill; to destroy
sleigh—*(n.)* a vehicle on runners

They uncovered a plot to *slay* their leader.
A *sleigh* glides over hard-packed snow.

sleight—*(n.)* skill with tricks
slight—*(adj.)* thin, small, light; *(v.)* to neglect or snub

The magician achieved his *sleight* of hand with a *slight* twist of
his wrist.

slew—*(v.)* past of slay; *(n.)* a large number
slough—*(n.)* a marshy pool of water
slue—*(v.)* to turn; to rotate

A *slew* of tree frogs live by the *slough* near my house.
A sail with roller rigging should *slue* easily.

soar—*(v.)* to rise high; to fly like a bird
sore—*(adj.)* painful; annoyed

Ignoring his *sore* ankle, the skater began to *soar* across the ice.

soared—*(v.)* flew like a bird; rose high
sword—*(n.)* a weapon with a long, sharp blade

The applause *soared* as the performers took their final bow.
He drew his *sword* in defiance.

sole—*(n.)* the bottom of a foot or shoe; a fish; *(adj.)* one and only

soul—*(n.)* the spirit; the vital part; a person

She was his *sole* survivor and inherited everything.
He was remembered as a merry, old *soul*.

soled—*(v.)* supplied the shoe's bottom; *(adj.)* of the sole

sold—*(v.)* did sell

The store *sold* thick-*soled* boots for climbing.

some—*(adv.)* about; a bit; *(adj.)* several; any; *(pron.)* a few

sum—*(n.)* the total

Some, but not all, of the math students arrived at the same *sum*.

son—*(n.)* a male offspring
sun—*(n.)* the bright center of the solar system

The *sun* came from behind a cloud as his *son* walked toward him.

spade—*(n.)* a tool for digging
spayed—*(v.)* neutered an animal

She turned the earth with a *spade*.
We *spayed* our adopted cat.

staid—*(adj.)* proper; sober; sedate
stayed—*(v.)* remained; propped up; stopped the action of a court

Impressed by the *staid* atmosphere in the museum, the children *stayed* quietly together.

stairs—*(n.)* steps
stares—*(n.)* fixed looks

Ignoring the *stares* of the crowd, the eager fan ran up the *stairs* to greet her idol.

stake—*(n.)* a pointed post; a wager; a share; *(v.)* to gamble; to mark
steak—*(n.)* a slice of meat or fish

They cooked the *steak* by spearing it with a *stake* they had cut from a tree.

stationary—*(adj.)* motionless; fixed
stationery—*(n.)* writing paper

A *stationary* bike is one way to exercise.
Her *stationery* was monogrammed with her initials.

steal—*(v.)* to rob; to smuggle; to move or act secretly
steel—*(n.)* a hard metal

The thieves were able to open a *steel* safe and *steal* the contents.

step—*(n.)* a stair; a single movement; a short distance; a level or degree; *(v.)* to walk a short distance
steppe—*(n.)* a broad, treeless plain

Step to the window of the train and see a vast, bare *steppe* roll by.

stile—*(n.)* a set of steps over a fence
style—*(n.)* a manner; the fashion; characteristics; *(v.)* to design

The *stile* was built in a rustic *style* with rough-hewn logs as steps.

straight—*(adj.)* even; direct; honest; in order; *(adv.)* virtuously; honestly
strait—*(n.)* a narrow waterway between two large bodies of water

We made a *straight* passage through the *strait* between the ocean and the sea.

straightened—*(v.)* made orderly; improved
straitened—*(v.)* limited; restricted due to financial difficulties

We felt relief after our *straitened* circumstances *straightened* out.

succor—*(n.)* aid; *(v.)* to help
sucker—*(n.)* a lollipop; a victim; the shoot of a plant; a small
  fish

  The church tries to provide *succor* for the poor and homeless.
  The bank teller offered a *sucker* to the customer's child.

suede—*(n.)* a soft, napped finish for cloth or leather
swayed—*(v.)* moved; influenced

  The quality of the *suede* in the coat *swayed* her to make the
  big purchase.

suite—*(n.)* connected rooms; a set of furniture
sweet—*(adj.)* sugary; pleasing; amiable; fresh; beloved;
  fragrant

  She sprayed a *sweet* air freshener throughout the *suite* of
  rooms.

summary—*(n.)* a brief outline; *(adj.)* direct; prompt; often
  impatient
summery—*(adj.)* of, like, or appropriate for summer

  He wrote a *summary* of the chapter.
  Her floral dress was light and *summery*.

sundae—*(n.)* an ice cream dessert; a topping
Sunday—*(n.)* a day of the week following Saturday

  On each *Sunday*, after the movie, we were treated to a *sundae*.

symbol—*see* cymbal

tacked—*(v.)* changed course; stitched loosely; pinned
tact—*(n.)* a keen sense and skill in what to do or say;
　　diplomacy

　　Using great *tact*, he *tacked* on an addition to the agreement.

tacks—*(n.)* small nails; *(v.)* pins; changes course; stitches
　　loosely
tax—*(n.)* a payment; a burden; *(v.)* to levy

　　Using four *tacks*, she posted a notice about the new *tax*.

tail—*(n.)* the hind end; a streaming from behind; *(v.)* to follow
tale—*(n.)* a story; a lie

　　The ancient *tale* told how the peacock got its magnificent *tail*.

taper—*(n.)* a thin candle; a gradual decrease; *(v.)* to lessen;
　　to become smaller
tapir—*(n.)* a large, hoglike animal

　　The snout of the *tapir* has a slight *taper* toward the end.

taro—*(n.)* a stemless, tropical plant with broad leaves
tarot—*(n.)* cards for telling fortunes

　　Poi, a staple of early Hawaiians, is made from *taro* root.
　　A *tarot* deck has 22 cards.

tarry—*(v.)* to linger or loiter; to wait
terry—*(n.)* a looped cotton fabric

She asked me to *tarry* while she dried herself with a *terry* cloth towel.

taught—*(v.)* was educated; did teach
taut—*(adj.)* tightly stretched; strained; in good condition; tidy; trim

Trainees in the Navy are *taught* to keep a *taut* ship.

taupe—*(n.)* a moderately dark brownish gray
tope—*(v.)* to drink liquor habitually and to excess; *(n.)* a small shark

The drunkard in the *taupe*-colored shirt began to *tope* at noon.

tea—*(n.)* a drink; an afternoon party
tee—*(n.)* a small golf peg; the place to start playing a hole on the golf course; a short-sleeved knitted shirt

From the first *tee*, she could see her friends having *tea* on the club porch.

team—*(n.)* two or more horses; a group working or playing together
teem—*(v.)* to abound or swarm; to pour into

The stands *teem* with loyal fans when the home *team* plays.

tear—*(n.)* a salty drop from the eye
tier—*(n.)* a row of seats; a level or layer

Sitting in the second *tier*, she shed a *tear* for the heroine.

teas—*(n.)* drinks made from soaking leaves from plants
tease—*(v.)* to mock; to torment

Her brother liked to *tease* her.

tens—*(n.)* multiples of ten
tends—*(v.)* takes care of; inclines toward

A beginning math student *tends* to confuse *tens* and ones.

tense—*(adj.)* strained; feeling or showing tension;
(n.) the time of a verb
tents—*(n.)* shelters made of canvas

The trip left them tired and *tense* until they settled in their *tents*.

tern—*(n.)* a gull-like seabird
turn—*(v.)* to rotate; to wrench; to move around; to change;
(n.) a chance

Watch the graceful *tern* wheel and *turn* above the waves!

their—*(pron.)* belonging to them
there—*(adv.)* in or at that place
they're—*(contr.)* they are; they were

They're hoping that *their* flight will arrive *there* in time to make connections.

threw—*(v.)* tossed; upset; sent rapidly
through—*(adv.)* from end to end; *(adj.)* finished; *(prep.)* past;
beyond

Despite injuries, she got *through* the game and *threw* 20 baskets.

Napoleon was **thrown** off his **throne** after losing support in France.

throes—*(n.)* spasms of pain; struggles; agony
throws—*(v.)* pitches; sends rapidly

Even in the *throes* of pain, she *throws* very accurately.

throne—*(n.)* a ruler's chair; a king's power
thrown—*(v.)* have, has, or was pitched

Napoleon was *thrown* off his *throne* after losing support in France.

thyme—*(n.)* a minty herb
time—*(n.)* a measure of duration; every moment; past, present, and future; a set period

Late summer is the *time* to freeze or dry sprigs of *thyme*.

tic—*(n.)* a spasm; twitches
tick—*(n.)* a small blood-sucking insect; a clicking sound

A facial *tic* can be annoying.
The deer *tick* carries Lyme disease.

tide—*(n.)* the rise and fall of the seas; a trend; *(v.)* to flow or carry
tied—*(v.)* bound; fastened

The rising *tide* of opposition left him *tied* to an unpopular cause.

tigress—*(n.)* a female tiger
Tigris—*(n.)* a river in Asia

The *tigress* was ferried across the *Tigris* to her new home in the zoo.

tilde—*(n.)* a diacritical mark used in Spanish and Portuguese
tilled—*(v.)* plowed; cultivated; labored

The *tilde* indicates a nasal sound for pronouncing the word.
They *tilled* the fields before planting them.

to—*(adv.)* forward; *(prep.)* because; until; along with; so as to reach; on; at; into; toward
too—*(adv.)* more than enough; also; very
two—*(adj.)(n.)* one more than one

It may not be *too* wise *to* visit relatives with *two* sick children.

toad—*(n.)* an amphibious animal
toed—*(adj.)* having toes; *(v.)* stood; walked; kicked
towed—*(v.)* pulled; hauled; dragged

A fat *toad* hopped across the road.
The two-*toed* sloth is slow moving.
My car was *towed* to the garage.

toe—*(n.)* a digit on the foot; the front of a shoe or sock; *(v.)* to touch, kick or strike

tow—*(v.)* to haul or drag; *(n.)* something dragged; fiber of flax, hemp, or jute; a head of pale, yellow hair

> He stuck his *toe* in the pool to test the water temperature. They had to *tow* their lively children away from the pool.

told—*(v.)* informed; said

tolled—*(v.)* rang slowly

> We were *told* that the bell *tolled* on the hour from 8 A.M. to 6 P.M. daily.

tool—*(n.)* a handheld instrument; a means of accomplishing a purpose; a person manipulated by another for a purpose

tulle—*(n.)* a netlike fabric

> The *tool* of her success was the creative way she used *tulle* in her dress designs.

tort—*(n.)* a wrongful act resulting in injury to another's property or reputation

torte—*(n.)* a rich cake made with eggs and ground nuts

> The *tort* for which the chef was awarded damages occurred when his *torte* recipes were stolen.

tortuous—*(adj.)* winding and twisted

torturous—*(adj.)* causing pain and torture

> Concentrating on the *tortuous* mountain road became *torturous* after six hours of driving.

tracked—*(v.)* followed; traced

tract—*(n.)* a system of body parts; a stretch of land; a political paper

> The owners of the *tract* were *tracked* through records in the town hall.

troop—*(n.)* a unit of scouts or soldiers; *(v.)* to walk together
troupe—*(n.)* a group of singers or actors; *(v.)* to travel as a
group

Troop Three awarded badges at their meeting yesterday.
A *troupe* from the city will sing *La Boheme* on Saturday.

trussed—*(v.)* tied up; supported
trust—*(n.)* confidence; hope; faith; care; custody; a monopoly;
property held for a beneficiary

The turkey was stuffed and *trussed*, then roasted in a moderate
oven.
She occupies a position of *trust* in the firm.

tucks—*(n.)* small pleats; *(v.)* covers snugly; fits securely
tux—*(n.)* *(informal)* a tuxedo, semiformal evening dress for a
man

The shirt for a *tux* usually has *tucks* on the front.

undo—*(v.)* to untie; to do away with; to ruin
undue—*(adj.)* too much; improper

You can't *undo* the result of applying *undue* pressure on a big balloon.

use—*see* ewes

urn—*see* earn

vain—*(adj.)* proud; conceited; worthless; futile

vane—*(n.)* a wind direction indicator; the blade of a turbine or windmill

vein—*(n.)* a blood vessel; a mineral deposit; the rib of a leaf or an animal's wing

> Their *vain* efforts to impress us were ludicrous.
> The weather *vane* was mounted on the barn.
> The tests revealed a rich *vein* of iron ore.

valance—*(n.)* a window treatment

valence—*(n.)* a number accompanying each chemical element

> The *valance* was covered with the drapery fabric.
> A *valence* is the number of binding sites on a molecule.

vale—*(n.)* a valley; earthly life; this world

veil—*(n.)* a light fabric cover; *(v.)* to hide or conceal

> The *vale* surrounding the river was hidden in a *veil* of mist.

vary—*(v.)* to change; to alter; to make different

very—*(adv.)* extremely; truly; really

> A *very* skilled tennis player will *vary* his serve.

venous—*(adj.)* having or composed of a vein or veins
Venus—*(n.)* an ancient goddess; a beautiful woman;
      the second planet from the sun

Venous blood is oxygen-poor.
The Romans called Aphrodite *Venus*.

verses—*(n.)* the plural of verse
versus—*(prep.)* against; as compared to

Her *verses* are inspired, *versus* all others we read today.

vial—*(n.)* a small glass bottle
vile—*(adj.)* wicked; disgusting
viol—*(n.)* any of several stringed instruments played with a
      bow

The *vial* of poison was an important clue in the *vile* crime.
She plays the bass *viol* exceedingly well.

vice—*(n.)* an evil habit or conduct; a fault or failing
vise (vice)—*(n.)* a device that holds firmly

His *vice* holds him like a *vise* from which he's unable to escape.

villain—*(n.)* a scoundrel; a criminal; an evildoer
villein—*(n.)* a serf who had the privileges of a freedman

A feudal lord was a *villain* if he ignored the rights of a *villein*.

wade—*(v.)* to walk through water; to proceed with difficulty
weighed—*(v.)* measured the weight; chose carefully; evaluated

> Before they began to *wade* across the stream, they *weighed* their chances of slipping on the rocks.

wail—*(v.)* to make a loud, long cry of grief or pain;
    (n.) a mournful cry
whale—*(n.)* a large sea mammal

> The dog gave a plaintive *wail* when it discovered the beached *whale*.

Because of his **weight** the elephant had to **wait** for the next elevator.

waist—*(n.)* a part of the body; a vest
waste—*(v.)* to ruin; to squander; to wear away; to dwindle; *(n.)* decay; neglect; refuse; left over

His *waist* measures 36 inches.
We should try not to *waste* energy.

wait—*(v.)* to be ready; to stay for; to remain; to serve food; to postpone or delay
weight—*(n.)* the amount of heaviness or importance; a heavy object

I can't *wait* until I lose some *weight*.

waive—*(v.)* to excuse, give up, defer
wave—*(v.)* to move back and forth; *(n.)* an upsurge; an ocean swell

They hoped the school would *waive* some requirements for registration.
With a *wave* of his hand, the registrar dismissed them.

Wales—*(n.)* a peninsula of Great Britain
whales—*(n.)* large sea mammals

Whales are seldom sighted off the coast of *Wales*.

want—*(v.)* to wish for; to feel a need or desire for; to require;
    (n.) the need
wont—*(adj.)* accustomed; *(n.)* usual practice, habit;
    (v.) accustom

I would not *want* to marry one who's *wont* to rise at dawn.

wares—*(n.)* merchandise for sale; pottery
wears—*(v.)* on the body; bears evidence of use; holds up;
    displays

The way she *wears* her colorful *wares* attracts buyers to her
booth.

warn—*(v.)* to caution; to tell of coming danger
worn—*(v.)* used as clothing; shows use; tired

An unusual noise may *warn* you that your brake pads are *worn*
thin.

way—*(n.)* the road, path, course, method
weigh—*(v.)* to measure heaviness; to evaluate

We're told the *way* to *weigh* less is to eat less and exercise
more.

we—*(pron.)* persons speaking or writing
wee—*(adj.)* tiny; very early

We returned from the party in the *wee* hours of morning.

weak—*(adj.)* lacking strength; feeble
week—*(n.)* seven days in a row

They had a *weak* excuse for being a *week* late with their rent.

wear—*(v.)* to have on; to show; to impair by use; to irritate
where—*(adv.)* in, at, or from what place

Where would one *wear* a top hat and tails?

weather—*(n.)* conditions of temperature, wind, and humidity;
　　　(v.) to survive
whether—*(conj.)* if it be the case; in case; in either case

The *weather* will determine *whether* or not we ski this weekend.

weave—*(v.)* to make by interlacing; to twist or spin;
　　　(n.) the texture
we've—*(contr.)* we have

We've come to watch you *weave* at your loom.

we'd—*(contr.)* we had; we would
weed—*(n.)* a plant that grows wild; *(v.)* to remove weeds

We'd pulled every *weed* from the garden before the rain started.

we'll—*(contr.)* we will; we shall
wheel—*(n.)* a round, turning device; *(v.)* to turn or move by
　　　way of wheels

With a good driver at the *wheel, we'll* get there safely.

whet—*(v.)* to sharpen
wet—*(adj.)* moistened, covered, or soaked with water

The *wet* weather did little to *whet* our appetite for a picnic.

which—*(pron.)* what one; that one
witch—*(n.)* a sorceress; an ugly, old woman

The house in *which* the young *witch* lived was full of bats and
mice.

while—*(conj.)* during a time; although; *(n.)* a period of time; *(v.)* to spend time

wile—*(n.)* a trick to fool, trap, or entice; *(v.)* to entice or lure

> *While* TV may *wile* you away from study, music may help you attend.

whine—*(v.)* to complain; *(n.)* a high-pitched sound

wine—*(n.)* a drink made from fermented grape juice

> The puppy began to *whine* as soon as we left the room.
> She poured the *wine* into long-stemmed glasses.

whole—*see* hole

wholly—*see* holy

When we left the room, the dog began to **whine**.

whoop—*see* hoop

who's—*(contr.)* who is; who has
whose—*(pron.)* belonging to who or which

> *Who's* going to listen to someone *whose* honesty is questionable?

wind—*(v.)* to change direction; to take a bending course; to coil or twine
wined—*(v.)* drank or served wine

> After an evening in which they were generously *wined*, they decided to *wind* their way home.

won—*see* one

wood—*(n.)* lumber; timber
would—*(v.)* is, are, or was willing

> We *would* like to have a big supply of *wood* cut before winter comes.

wrap—*see* rap

wrapped—*see* rapped

wreak—*see* reek

wrest—*see* rest

wretch—*see* retch

wright—*see* right

wring—*see* ring

write—*see* right

wrote—*see* rote

wrung—*see* rung

wry—*see* rye

Our neighbor planted a hedge of **yews**.

yew—*see* ewe

yews—*see* use

yoke—*(n.)* a wooden harness for oxen; bondage; *(v.)* to join
    together; to harness
yolk—*(n.)* the yellow part of an egg

    The peasants revolted and threw off the *yoke* of serfdom.
    The egg I broke has a double *yolk*.

you—*see* ewe

you'll—*(contr.)* you will; you shall
yule—*(n.)* Christmas; the season of Christmas

    You'll be asked to attend many parties during the *Yule*tide.

your—*(pron.)* belonging to or done by you
you're—*(contr.)* you are

    If *you're* able, *your* friends all hope you will join them.

Bibliography

Ellyson, Louise. *A Dictionary of Homonyms.* Banner Books International, Sherman Oaks, California, 1977.

Lass, Abraham and Betty. *Dictionary of Pronunciation.* Quadrangle/The New York Times Book Co., New York, 1976.

Merriam Webster Collegiate Dictionary. 10th ed. 1994.

Presson, Leslie. *What in the World Is a Homophone?* Barron's Educational Series, Inc., Hauppauge, New York, 1996.

Random House Webster's College Dictionary. 1995.

Webster's New World Dictionary. 3d. ed. 1990.

Wilson, Kenneth G. *The Columbia Guide to Standard American English.* Columbia University Press, New York, 1993.